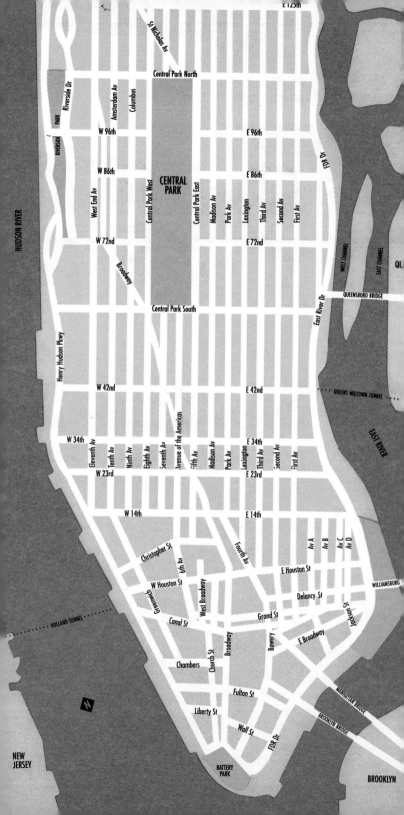

SPADE & ARCHER'S

50 MAPS

of

NEW YORK

With Contributions from
Geoffrey Holder, Thomas Hoving,
Martha Stewart, Fred Lebow,
Timothy White and others.

Produced by Spade & Archer, Inc.
New York

H.M. Gousha
A Division of Simon & Schuster Inc.
A Paramount Communications Company

New York

© 1990 by Spade & Archer, Inc.:
J. C. Suarès,
Dominique Bluhdorn, and
Stephen D. Kaplan.
All rights reserved.

Text: Randall de Sève
Design: Christy Trotter
Basic New York Map:
    Janine Leib
Research: Megan Ratner,
    Ann Lewis, Geraldine
    Bertolini
Copy Editing:
    Catherine Schurdak
Production: Gates Studio

ISBN 0-13-321746-9

Published by H.M. Gousha,
A Division of Simon & Schuster Inc.,
A Paramount Communications
Company.

Printed in America. First Edition.

CONTENTS

1 WHERE TO RENT A BIKE

On weekends throughout the year Central Park is closed to auto traffic. What better way to savor the day than to bike the loop—bundled up in winter for a vigorous six-mile sprint, or dressed-down in summer for a lazy ride in the sun?

1   AAA Central Park Bicycle Rentals
Loeb Boathouse at 74th St.
861-4137
Rentals March-November only.

2   A West Side Bicycle Store
231 West 96th St.
663-7531

3   Canal St. Bicycles
417 Canal St.
334-8000

4   City Cycles
659 Broadway
254-4757
Rentals March-September only.

5   Country Cycling Tours
140 West 83rd St.
874-5151
Closed weekends October-March.

6   Eddie's Bicycles Shop
490 Amsterdam Ave.
580-2011

7   Gene's 79th St. Discounted Bicycles
242 East 79th St.
249-9218

8   Larry & Jeff's Bicycle Plus
204 East 85th St.
794-2201

9   Metro Bicycle Discount House
332 East 14th St.
228-4344

10 Metro Bicycles
1311 Lexington Ave.
427-4450

11 Metro Sixth Ave. Bicycles
546 Sixth Ave.
255-5100

12 Midtown Bicycles
360 West 47th St.
581-4500

13 Pedal Pushers Bicycle Shop
1306 Second Ave.
288-5592
Closed Tuesdays.

NOTE: All rental shops require identification (driver's license or equivalent) and a major credit card or a substantial cash deposit.

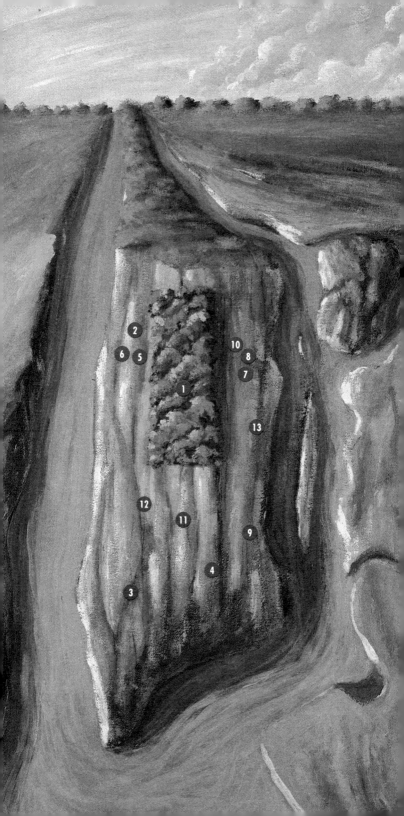

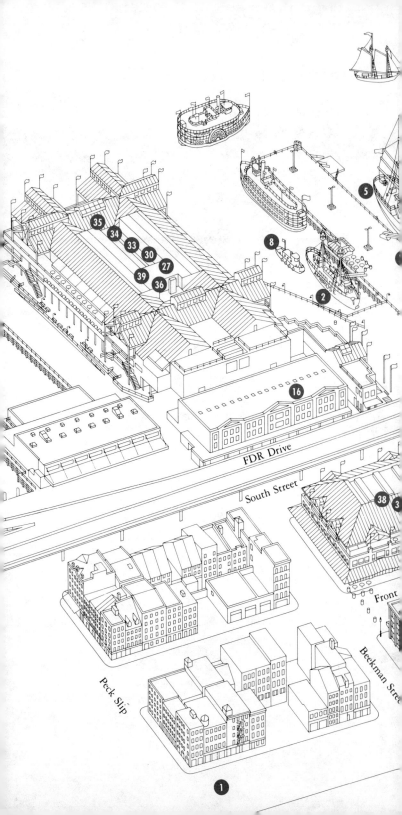

FDR Drive

South Street

Front

Peck Slip

Beekman Street

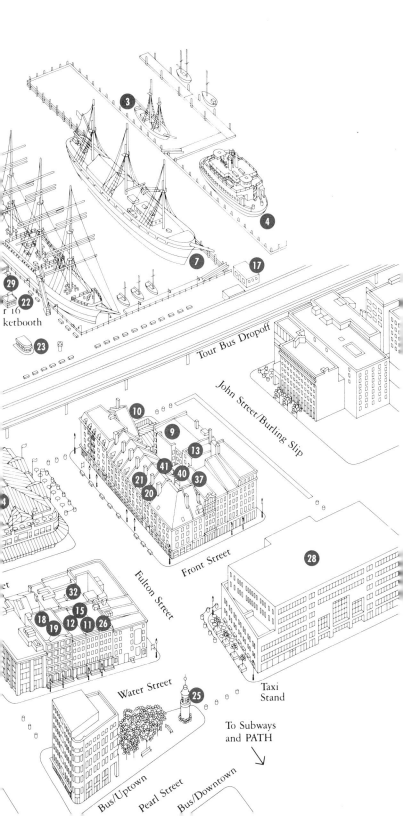

3

4

7

17

29

22

r 16
ketbooth

23

Tour Bus Dropoff

John Street/Burling Slip

10

9

13

41

40

37

21

20

Front Street

28

32

Fulton Street

18

15

19   12   11   26

Water Street

25

Taxi
Stand

To Subways
and PATH

Bus/Uptown

Pearl Street   Bus/Downtown

2 THE SOUTH STREET SEAPORT

1 CAPTAIN ROSE HOUSE
273 Water St.

HISTORIC SHIPS

2 *Ambrose*

3 *Lettie G. Howard*

4 *Major General William H. Hart*

5 *Peking*

6 *Pioneer*

7 *Wavertree*

8 *W.O. Decker*

MUSEUMS

9 A. A. Low Building, Norway Galleries

10 Boat Building Shop

11 Book & Chart Store

12 Bowne & Co., Stationers

13 Children's Center

14 Container Store

15 Curiosity Shop

16 Fulton Fish Market

17 Maritime Crafts Center

18 Melville Library

19 Museum Gallery

20 Museum Shop

21 Museum Visitors' Center

22 Pier 16 Ticket Booth

23 The Pilothouse

24 Small Craft Collection

25 *Titanic* Memorial Lighthouse

26 Waterfront Photographer

RESTAURANTS

27 Café Café
Pier 17
406-2870
Light American fare.

28 Cafe Fledermaus
199 Water St.
269-5890
Austrian.

29 Container Cafe
Pier 16
943-1350
Basically Burgers.

30 Fluties Pier 17
19 Fulton St.
693-0777
Seafood.

31 Fulton St. Cafe
19 Fulton St.
227-2288
Mostly seafood.

32 Gianni's
15 Fulton St.
608-7300
Northern Italian.

33 Harbour Lights
Pier 17
227-2800
Continental.

34 Jade Sea
Pier 17
285-0505
Chinese.

35 Liberty Cafe
Pier 17
406-1111
Continental with Italian flair.

36 Mobile
Pier 17
619-4800
Cajun.

37 North Star Pub
93 South St.
406-4531
British pub.

38 Roebling's Grille
11 Fulton St.
227-9322
American.

39 Sgarlato's Cafe
Pier 17
619-5226
Italian.

40 Sloppy Louie's
92 South St.
509-9694
Seafood.

41 Sweet's
2 Fulton St.
344-8189
Seafood.

For general information on The South Street Seaport call 732-7678

THE CENTRAL PARK ZOO

Reopened in 1988 after 5 years and an over $35 million renovation, the new Central Park Zoo is now managed by the New York Zoological Society. In keeping with the Society's commitment to conservation, education, and the principles of wildlife exhibition (only animals that can be properly cared for are at the zoo), the zoo has recreated the animals' natural habitats in 3 climatic areas: the Tropic Zone, the Temperate Territory, and the Polar Circle.

1 TROPIC ZONE

Monkeys, Snakes, Tortoises, Lizards, Poison Frogs, Toucans, Piranhas, Fighting Fish.

2 TEMPERATE TERRITORY

Sea Lions, Red Pandas, Japanese Macaques, Turtles.

3 POLAR CIRCLE

Polar Bears, Seals, Arctic Foxes, Penguins.

4 Central Garden
Sea Lion pool.

5 Intelligence Garden

6 Zoo cafe

The Central Park Zoo is at Fifth Avenue and 64th St. Open 10am-5pm, M-F; Sat, Sun, and holidays, until 5:30pm from April-October. The Zoo closes at 4:30pm every day from November-March. May-September the Zoo closes at 8pm on Tue evenings. For general information on the Central Park Zoo call 439-6538 weekdays or the New York Zoological Society at 367-1010 (recorded announcement).

4 BEST THINGS FRENCH

New York has always been a subject of great fascination for the French. A Frenchman's first impression of New York lies in the modern appearance of the city, then he discovers how many different areas of New York are, in fact, little villages themselves.

ANDRÉ JAMMET, *Owner,* La Caravelle

1 Alliance Francaise
22 East 60th St.
355-6100
French language instruction and cultural events.

2 Baccarat, Inc.
625 Madison Ave.
826-4100
Crystal.

3 Cartier and Les Must de Cartier
653 Fifth Ave.
753-0111
Jewelry.

4 Chanel
5 East 57th St.
355-5050
Fashion and accessories.

5 Charles Jourdan
Trump Tower
725 Fifth Ave.
644-3830
6 769 Madison Ave.
628-0133
Shoes.

7 D. Porthault
18 East 69th St.
688-1660
Linens.

8 French Embassy
972 Fifth Ave.
570-4400
For information on French cultural events throughout New York City contact the Department of Cultural Services.

9 Givenchy
1020 Madison Ave.
517-8900
Men's clothing.

10 Hermès
11 East 57th St.
751-3181
Accessories.

11 Librairie de France
Rockefeller Center
610 Fifth Ave.
581-8810
Bookstore.

12 Louis Vuitton
51 East 57th St.
371-6111
Luggage.

13 Parker Meridien
119 West 56th St.
245-5000
Hotel.

14 Pierre Deux
870 Madison Ave.
570-9343
15 369 Bleecker St.
243-7740
China, fabrics, housewares, and antiques.

16 Plaza Athénéé
37 East 64th St.
734-9100
Hotel.

17 Puiforcat
811 Madison Ave.
734-3838
Silver.

18 Regine's
502 Park Ave.
826-0990
Nightclub.

19 Stephane Kelian
702 Madison Ave.
980-1919
Shoes.

20 Van Cleef & Arpels
744 Fifth Ave.
644-9500
Jewelry.

5 BEST FRENCH DISHES

Compiled with the participation of many of New York's top restaurant owners, mâitre d's, chefs, and food writers, this dish finder is an index to some of Manhattan's best French cuisine.

1 Boneless quail stuffed with mushrooms in a crust with truffle sauce
La Côte Basque
5 East 55th St.
688-6525

2 Bouillabaisse with lobster
La Colombe d'Or
134 East 26th St.
689-0666

3 Bourride, a fish stew with aiolli
Provence
38 MacDougal St.
475-7500
Bistro.

4 Cassoulet
Quatorze
240 West 14th St.
206-7006
Bistro.

5 Chocolate soufflé with Grand Marnier sauce
La Grenouille
3 East 52nd St.
752-1495

6 Couscous Mediterranée aux crevettes
Le Refuge
166 East 82nd St.
861-4505

7 Crusty roast chicken and garlicky potato pie
Chez Louis
1016 Second Ave.
752-1400
Bistro.

8 Fallen chocolate soufflé cake
Chanterelle
2 Harrison St.
966-6960

9 Filet of sole catalan
Lutèce
249 East 50th St.
752-2225

10 Galanga, shitaki broth with shrimp dumplings
Lafayette
65 East 56th St.
832-1565

11 Gigot in spinach sauce with fresh herbs
La Caravelle
33 West 55th St.
586-4252

12 Grilled red snapper with a soy butter sauce
Le Regence
37 East 64th St.
606-4647

13 Grilled salmon
Cafe Luxembourg
200 West 70th St.
873-7411

14 Lavender honey glazed organic duckling with roast shallots
Bouley
165 Duane St.
608-3852

15 Lobster sautéed in whiskey sauce
René Pujol
321 West 51st St.
246-3023

16 Marinated smoked salmon with warm potato salad
La Cité
120 West 51st St.
956-7100
Bistro.

17 Mille feuilles of salmon and potatoes with cream of dill
La Gauloise
502 Sixth Ave.
691-1363
Bistro.

18 Parmesan soufflé
La Tulipe
104 West 13th St.
691-8860
Bistro.

19 Pot-au-feu
Café des Artistes
1 West 67th St.
877-3500

20 Poulet rôti aux pommes frites
Poiret
474 Columbus Ave.
724-6880

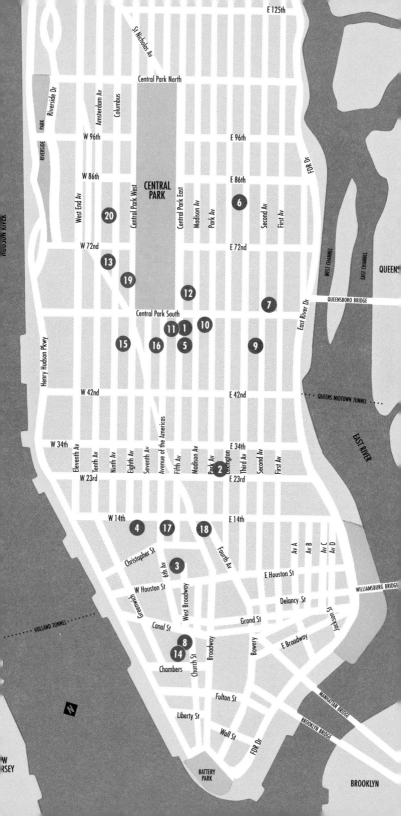

TRIBECA GALLERIES AND RESTAURANTS

If you thought it was still hip to be square, take a look at the triangle below Canal Street.

Once an industrial neighborhood, TriBeCa's large ex-warehouse and factory buildings have attracted some of the city's most interesting artists and performers—who have, in turn, lured the downtown restaurant and gallery scene their way. A few places worth noting:

GALLERIES

1 48 Laight Gallery
48 Laight St.
505-9668
Contemporary art.

2 The Alternative Museum
17 White St.
966-4444
Experimental music concerts; poetry readings; contemporary art with political content.

3 Artists' Space
223 West Broadway
226-3970
Emerging artists, videos, and films.

4 Ceres Gallery
91 Franklin St.
226-4725
Art by women.

5 The Clocktower
108 Leonard St.
13th Floor
233-1096
Contemporary art.

6 Neo Persona Gallery
51 Hudson St.
406-9835
Features local TriBeCa artists.

7 Pelavin Editions
13 Jay St.
925-9424
Mostly works on paper: etchings, lithographs, monotypes.

8 Soho Photo Gallery
15 White St.
226-8571
Photo artistry.

9 Thomas St. Cafe & Gallery
8 Thomas St.
349-6350
An 1874 cast iron-front, landmark-designated building that houses a gallery of local artists in an Italian-American restaurant.

10 Walking Art/Nakazawa Studio
28 Hubert St.
226-5336
Japanese art clothing.

11 White Columns
142 Christopher St.
924-4212
Contemporary art.

BEST RESTAURANTS

12 Alison on Dominick St.
38 Dominick St.
727-1188
Southwestern French cuisine.

13 Arqua Ristorante
281 Church St.
334-1888
Homemade pastas, grilled fish and meat.

14 Bouley
165 Duane St.
608-3852
Classical French.

15 Capsouto Frères
451 Washington St.
966-4900
Classical French cuisine.

16 Chanterelle
6 Harrison St.
966-6960
Formal French. Reserve well in advance.

17 Montrachet
239 West Broadway
219-2777
Modern French.

18 The Odeon
145 West Broadway
233-0507
French Bistro.

19 TriBeCa Grill
375 Greenwich St.
941-3900
Modern grill menu.

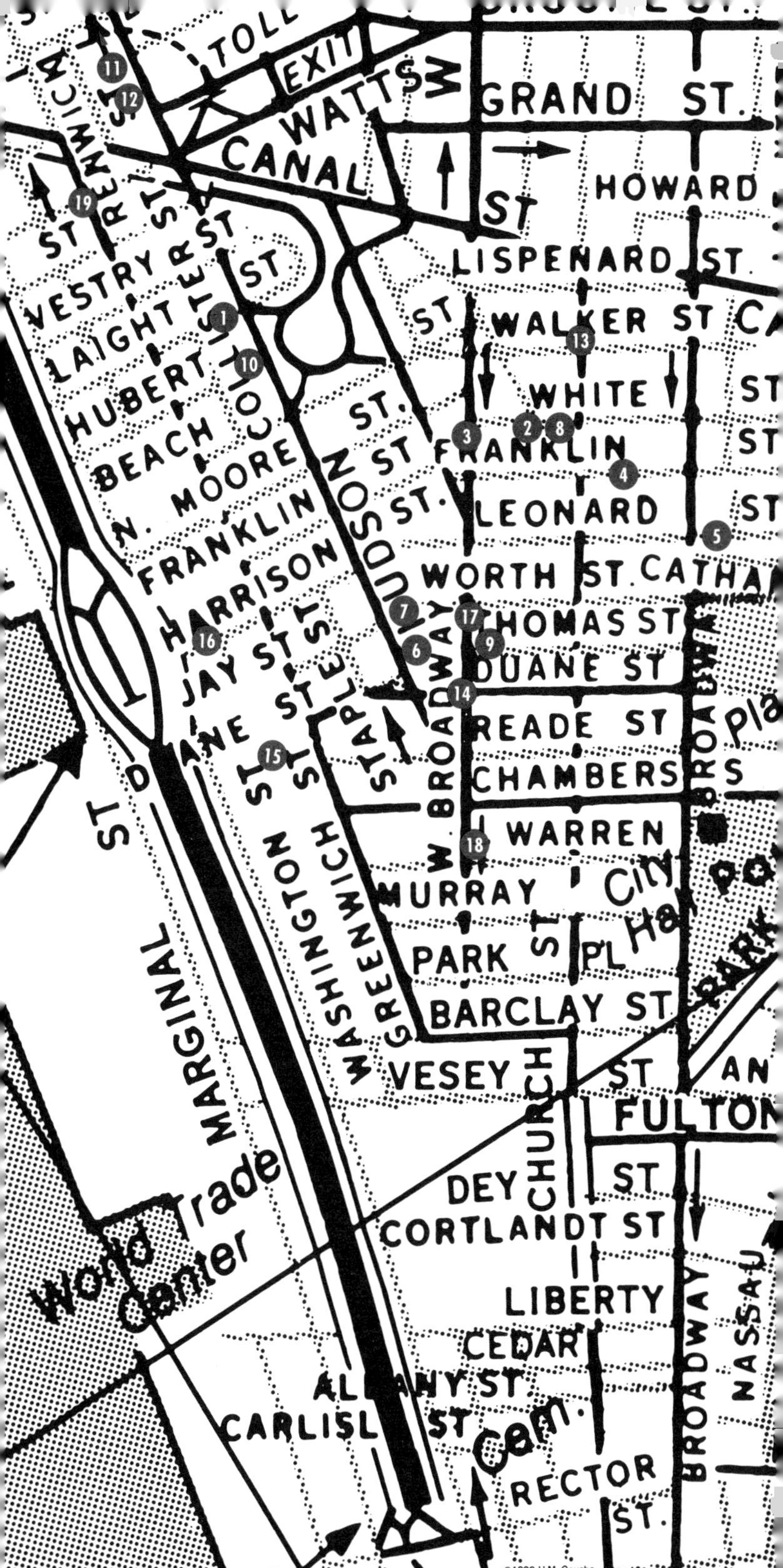

7 MUSIC NOTES I (Shops)

New York City is rock and roll's grittiest laboratory. It's the place where Tin Pan Alley spawned Brill Building Pop; where Atlantic, Columbia and RCA Records carved out their turf; where Bob Dylan inspired Paul Simon; where Billy Joel forged a peppery hybrid from the Young Rascals, Sinatra saloon crooning and classic piano rock; where Lou Reed and John Cale created downtown primativism, and CBGB's made a home for Patti Smith, and Talking Heads; where Living Colour got loud; and where hip-hop and rap made the world safe for the new jack swing. In sum, Manhattan rock reverberates with the restless ballet of the streets.

TIMOTHY WHITE, *Rock Critic, Author,* Rock Stars *and* Catch A Fire—The Life of Bob Marley

1 The Island Trading Company
15 East 4th St.
Sells handsome West Indian art and handicrafts, plus the best vintage reggae from Bob Marley and the Wailers to Burning Spear.

2 It's Only Rock and Roll
49 West 8th St.
2nd Floor
Looking for a back issue of CRAWDADDY? *A mint copy of Yoko Ono's* GRAPEFRUIT? *This is the depot you've dreamed of.*

3 Manny's Musical Instruments and Accessories
156 West 48th St.
Smack in the heart of the recording studio district, this is the machine shop and hardware headquarters of all strung-out and unstrung rockers of note.

4 Matt Umanov Guitars
273 Bleecker St.
The timeless Village chapel of acoustic axes. Matt has been providing Bob Dylan with customized guitars for decades.

5 Bleecker Bob's
118 West 3rd St.
Crusty counter service, but often-killer stock of punk and garage band obscurities.

6 Colony Records
1619 Broadway
On the ground floor of the storied Brill Building, this vinyl repository is an ample outlet of last resort.

7 J & R Music World
23 Park Row
Solid source of jazz across the spectrum.

8 The Music Factory
1476 Broadway
Manhattan's best treasure trove of old and new rap and hip-hop, from Kool Herc to Queen Latifah.

9 Revolver Records
45 West 8th St.
2nd Floor
Broad selection of out-of-print vinyl, especially Beatles and Brit rock.

10 Smash Compact Disks
17 St. Mark's Pl.
For CD epicureans hot to locate rare promo items and obsure CD3 imports.

11 St. Mark's Sounds
20 St. Mark's Pl.
Swell collectors' resource, especially when Binky Philips, Lower Manhattan's venerable guitar-rock cult hero, is there.

12 Tower Records
692 Broadway
The downtown beat bazaar. Flirt with other afficionados and buy a Young Rascals or Lou Reed CD.

13 Tower Records
1965 Broadway
Lincoln Center's record supermarket. Full of students cruising for pop distractions.

14 Vinylmania
30 Carmine St.
Primo outlet for dance music.

E 125th

St Nicholas Av

Central Park North

Riverside Dr

Amsterdam Av

Columbus

W 96th

E 96th

West End Av

Central Park West

W 86th

E 86th

CENTRAL PARK

Central Park East

Madison Av

Park Av

Lexington

Third Av

Second Av

First Av

W 72nd

E 72nd

WEST CHANNEL

EAST CHANNEL

QUEEN

Broadway

13

RIVERSIDE PARK

HUDSON RIVER

Henry Hudson Pkwy

Central Park South

QUEENSBORO BRIDGE

East River Dr

W 42nd

3
6
8

E 42nd

QUEENS MIDTOWN TUNNEL

EAST RIVER

W 34th

Eleventh Av

Tenth Av

Ninth Av

Eighth Av

Seventh Av

Avenue of the Americas

Fifth Av

Madison Av

Park Av

Lexington

Third Av

Second Av

First Av

E 34th

W 23rd

E 23rd

W 14th

E 14th

14

2
9

Christopher St.

6th Av

Fourth Av

Av A

Av B

Av C

Av D

10
11

1

4

12

5

E Houston St

Gansevoort

WILLIAMSBURG BRIDGE

Jackson St

Delancy St

West Broadway

Canal St

Grand St

Church St

Broadway

Bowery

E Broadway

HOLLAND TUNNEL

Chambers

7

Fulton St

MANHATTAN BRIDGE

Liberty St

BROOKLYN BRIDGE

Wall St

FDR Dr

BATTERY PARK

BROOKLYN

EW ERSEY

N

MUSIC NOTES II (Clubs)

1 Apollo Theater
253 West 125th St.
The legend roars on, in restored splendor, with plenty of rap, R&B, funk and classic soul to share. (And the top-balcony jury on talent nights remains ferocious.)

2 Beacon Theater
Broadway at 74th St.
Manhattan's last surviving rock palace, where elder statesmen and women split the footlights with the latest top 40 crop.

3 Bottom Line
15 West 4th St.
The original no-frills rock supper club, where Springsteen tangoed on the tables and Buster Poindexter holds court.

4 Cat Club
76 East 13th St.
Mecca for the mascaraed metal crowd, with acts like Enuff Z'Nuff and Electric Angels holding forth in all their tatty stridor.

5 CBGB and OMFUG
315 Bowery
The punk/old wave Lourdes, where Ramones, Patti Smith, and the Talking Heads cut their teeth, and Prong now packs 'em in.

6 Dan Lynch's
221 Second Ave.
A wise and welcoming urban blues club. Well worth an evening of beers, tears, and, assorted sage renditions of "Big Boss Man."

7 Kilimanjaro
531 West 19th St.
Damn good Afro-Pop parlor with the right amenity: room to dance.

8 Lismar Lounge
41 First Ave.
Reconstituted biker bar with ballsy leather 'n metal bands in the basement.

9 Lone Star Roadhouse
240 West 52nd St.
The best boots-up ginmill in Manhattan, featuring Texas rumble, honky-tonk country, saucy zydeco, swamp boogie, Tulsa roll, and ducktail rock.

10 Nell's
246 West 14th St.
Modern speak-easy in the smart and sedate mode. A fine site to converse over Cristal, swap bon-mots, and catch Nell's own slinky-sly shows.

11 Palladium
126 East 14th St.
Club MTV's over-designed ballroom for late-night hipsters and hobbled Lambada holdouts.

12 Pyramid
101 Ave. A bet. 6th and 7th Sts.
Top venue for outre performance artists (Karen Finley) and hardcore punks (Butthole Surfers).

13 The Ritz
254 West 54th St.
Tidier resurrection of the beloved downtown rock toilet. Often with live radio simulcasts.

14 Wetlands
161 Hudson St.
A rock saloon with vaguely leftist atmosphere and a great range of acts, including rappers, hard reggae, and rockin' country.

15 Woody's in the Village
82 East 4th St.
Rolling Stone Ron Wood's rock lounge. A likely joint for encountering an off-beat gem as well as a celebrity jam.

9 BARS: WINE, SCOTCH, BEER, AND CLASSICS

For a full body or fragrant bouquet, the Soho Kitchen offers close to 100 vintages, the widest selection of wines by the glass in the city. The North Star Pub stocks regional single-malt whiskeys, and a small reading library to ponder post-taste.

The Manhattan Brewing Company makes its own beer—seven varieties—and serves it with hamburgers and french fries under the massive brewing tanks.

WINE

1 Grapes
522 Columbus Ave.
362-3004

2 I Tre Merli
463 Broadway
254-8699

3 Lavin's
23 West 39th St.
921-1288

4 Novotel
226 West 52nd St.
315-0100

5 One Hudson Café
One Hudson St.
608-5835

6 Sofi
102 Fifth Ave.
463-8888

7 Soho Kitchen & Bar
103 Greene St.
925-1866

SCOTCH

8 Abbey Restaurant
237 West 105th St.
222-8713

9 Barrymore's
267 West 45th St.
391-8400

10 Churchill's
1277 Third Ave.
650-1618

11 Donahue's
770 Second Ave.
883-1193

12 Harry's New York Bar
Helmsley Palace
455 Madison Ave.
888-7000

13 The Landmark Tavern
626 Eleventh Ave.
757-8595

14 The North Star Pub
93 South St.
509-6757

BEER

15 Hanratty's
1754 Second Ave.
289-3200

16 Manhattan Brewing
Company
40 Thompson St.
219-9250

17 PJ Clarke's
915 Third Ave.
759-1650
Scotch also.

18 Rectangle's
159 Second Ave.
677-8410

CLASSICS

19 Algonquin Hotel Lounge
59 West 44th St.
840-6800

20 Bemelman's Bar
The Carlyle
35 East 76th St.
744-1600

21 Café des Artistes
1 West 67th St.
877-3500

22 Cedar Tavern
82 University Pl.
675-4449

23 Jockey Club
112 Central Park South
664-7700

24 McSorleys Old Ale House
15 East 7th St.
473-8800

25 The Oak Bar
The Plaza Hotel
Fifth Ave. at 59th St.

26 Peculier Pub
182 West 4th St.
691-8667

E 125th

St Nicholas Av

Central Park North

Riverside Dr

8

Amsterdam Av

Columbus

PARK

RIVERSIDE

W 96th

E 96th

15

West End Av

W 86th

E 86th

1

Central Park West

CENTRAL
PARK

Central Park East

20

Park Av

Lexington

10

Second Av

First Av

FDR Dr

HUDSON RIVER

W 72nd

E 72nd

Broadway

21

East River Dr

WEST CHANNEL

EAST CHANNEL

QUE

Queensboro Bridge

23 **25**

Henry Hudson Pkwy

4

9

12

17

East River Dr

13

19

QUEENS MIDTOWN TUNNEL

W 42nd

E 42nd

11

3

EAST RIVER

W 34th

W 34th Av

Eleventh Av

Tenth Av

Ninth Av

Eighth Av

Seventh Av

Avenue of the Americas

Madison Av

Park Av

Lexington

Third Av

Second Av

First Av

E 34th

6

W 23rd

E 23rd

W 14th

E 14th

22

24 **18**

Av A

Av B

Av C

Av D

Christopher St

6th Av

Fourth Av

26

E Houston St

WILLIAMSBURG BR

Greenwich

W Houston St

West Broadway

Delancy St

Jackson St

HOLLAND TUNNEL

16

7

Canal St

2

Grand St

Bowery

E Broadway

5

Church St

Broadway

MANHATTAN BRIDGE

Chambers

Fulton St

Liberty St

14

BROOKLYN BRIDGE

Wall St

FDR Dr

NEW
JERSEY

BATTERY
PARK

BROOKLYN

OPEN ALL NIGHT

One of the wonders of New York is that you are never very far from an open-all-night Korean grocery, deli, or Food Emporium supermarket.

It's all out there, whatever your need—from the locksmith to the vet—even at 3:00 a.m.

DRUG STORES
(No pharmacy services)

1 Love Discount
2030 Broadway
877-4141

2 Manhattan Love
2181 Broadway
595-7711

FOOD

3 Delmonico Gourmet
Food Market
55 East 59th St. bet. Park
and Madison Aves.
751-5559

**MAGAZINE STORES
AND NEWSSTANDS**

4 Gem Spa
131 Second Ave. at St.
Mark's Pl.
529-1146

5 Leightons Newsstand
Columbus Ave. at 81st St.
6 First Ave. at 63rd St.
7 Broadway at 50th St.

MESSENGER

8 Air Couriers
20 West 22nd St.
242-1160

PHARMACY

9 Kaufman Pharmacy
557 Lexington Ave.
755-2266

POST OFFICE

10 Main Post Office
Eighth Ave. at 33rd St.
967-8588

RESTAURANTS

11 Around the Clock Café
8 Stuyvesant St. just off
Third Ave.
598-0402
Soups, salads, pastas.

12 Brasserie
100 East 53rd St.
751-4840
Continental.

13 Empire Diner
210 Tenth Ave. at 22nd St.
243-2736
Diner traditionals and more.

14 Florent
69 Gansevoort St. near
Washington St.
989-5779
Bistro.

15 H & H Bagel
2239 Broadway at 80th St.
595-8000

16 Kiev International
117 Second Ave.
674-4040
Russian food.

17 Kossar's Bialy Bakery
367 Grand St.
473-4810

TRANSLATOR

18 All Language Services Inc.
545 Fifth Ave. at 45th St.
986-1688

VETERINARIANS

19 Animal Medical Center
510 East 62nd St.
838-8100

20 Dr. Paul Schwartz
250 East 73rd St.
628-4124

**WORD PROCESSING
AND CLERICAL HELP**

21 Around the Clock Staffing
235 West 56th St.
245-1750

©H.M. Gousha

10 BEST RESTAURANTS IN THE PROVINCES

When the press and crunch of concrete and asphalt get to you there is respite nearby.

Cross any bridge, take any tunnel, and you're on your way to the boroughs and beyond, where bucolic, gastronomic pleasures await.

BROOKLYN

1 Gage & Tollner Restaurant
372 Fulton St.
(718) 875-5181
111 years old, this is New York's oldest restaurant and the first to become a landmark. Superb Southern cuisine and seafood.

2 Peter Lugar's Restaurant
Broadway and Driggs Ave.
(718) 387-7400
Simply one of New York's best steakhouses.

3 River Café
Water St.
(718) 522-5200
Below the Brooklyn Bridge; one of the city's finest restaurants and views.

CONNECTICUT

4 The Elms Inn
500 Main St., Ridgefield
(203) 438-2541
Historic 1799 inn and tavern.

5 Stonehenge
Rte. 7, Ridgefield
(203) 438-6511
The dining room's picture windows overlook an idyllic pond.

LONG ISLAND

6 The American Hotel
Main Street, Sag Harbor
(516) 725-3535
Food and hotel—one of the Hampton's most famous; well worth the trip.

7 Sapore di Mare
Montauk Highway, Wainscott
(516) 537-2764
Pino Luongo's restaurant with an emphasis on seafood—many say the best in the Hamptons.

WESTCHESTER

8 Auberge Maxime
Ridgefield Rd., North Salem
(914) 669-5450
One of the best French restaurants anywhere located in this beautiful horse country.

9 The Box Tree
Rtes. 22 and 116, Purdys.
(914) 277-3677
Romantic country cousin of New York's reknowned Box Tree Restaurant.

10 La Cremaillère
Greenwich Rd., Banksville
4 miles from exit 31 on the Merritt Pkwy.
(914) 234-9647
This exquisite French restaurant close to Manhattan is a favorite for lunch in the country.

WORST PLANE CRASHES

1 July 28, 1945: Empire State Building, 34th St. at 5th Ave.
Army Air Force B-24 hits Empire State Building's 79th Floor, 13 killed.

2 December 17, 1951: Elizabeth, NJ
Non-Scheduled C-46 crashes into river, 56 killed.

3 January 22, 1952: Elizabeth, NJ
American Airlines Convair crashes into an apartment house, 31 killed.

4 February 11, 1952: Elizabeth, NJ
National DC-6 crashes into an apartment house, 22 killed.

5 April 5, 1952: Jamaica, NY north of Idlewild Airport
C-46 cargo plane crashes in a residential neighborhood, 5 killed.

6 February 2, 1957: Rikers Island
Northeast DC-6 crashes in snowstorm, 22 killed.

7 February 3, 1959: East River off LaGuardia Airport
American Electra crashes on landing approach, 65 killed.

8 December 16, 1960: Staten Island/Brooklyn
TWA Super Constellation and United DC-7 collide, all 128 aboard and six on the ground killed, (including a Christmas tree vendor).

9 March 1, 1962: Jamaica Bay south of Kennedy Airport
American 707 crashes, 95 killed.

10 February 9, 1965: Atlantic Ocean off Jones Beach
Eastern DC-7 crashes, 84 killed.

11 June 24, 1975: Rockaway Blvd. north of Kennedy Airport
Eastern 727 crashes, 113 killed.

12 May 16, 1977: Pan Am Heliport, Park Ave. at 44th St.
NY Airways Helicopter slides from rooftop heliport when landing gear collapses, 5 killed, including one pedestrian.

13 September 20, 1989: Rikers Island Channel off LaGuardia Airport
USAir 737 crashes on takeoff, 2 killed.

14 February 11, 1990: Cove Neck, Oyster Bay, Long Island
Avianca 707 crashes, 73 killed.

13 HERE TO STAY

New York gets in your blood—and for some, it's hard to leave.
Here are some well-known New Yorkers who never will:

1 BROOKLYN QUAKER CEMETERY
Prospect Park, Brooklyn
Montgomery Clift

2 EAST MARION, LONG ISLAND
Mark Rothko

3 FERNCLIFF CEMETERY
Hartsdale, Westchester
Joan Crawford
Judy Garland
Malcolm X
Thelonius Monk

4 FLUSHING CEMETERY
Flushing, Queens
Louis Armstrong

5 GATE OF HEAVEN CEMETERY
Hawthorne, Westchester
Jimmy Cagney
George Herman "Babe" Ruth

6 GRANT'S TOMB
Manhattan
Ulysses Grant

7 KENSICO CEMETERY
Valhalla, Westchester
Lou Gehrig
Sergei Rachmaninoff

8 HARTSDALE CANINE CEMETERY
Hartsdale, Westchester
John Barrymore's cat
Kate Smith's dog
Joe Garagiola's poodle

9 MT. OLIVET CEMETERY
Maspeth, Queens
Jack "Legs" Diamond

10 OAK HILL CEMETERY
Nyack
Joseph Cornell
Edward Hopper
Carson McCullers

11 OAKLAND CEMETERY
Sag Harbor, Long Island
George Balanchine

12 PINELAWN CEMETERY
Melville, Long Island
John Coltrane

13 SACRED HEART CEMETERY
Southampton, Long Island
Gary Cooper

14 SALEM FIELDS CEMETERY
Cypress Hills, Brooklyn
Peggy Guggenheim

15 SLEEPY HOLLOW, WESTCHESTER
Andrew Carnegie

16 ST. JAMES EPISCOPAL CEMETERY
St. James, Long Island
Stanford White

17 ST. RAYMOND'S CEMETERY
Tremont, Bronx
Billie Holiday

18 WESTCHESTER HILLS CEMETERY
Hastings-On-Hudson, Westchester
George Gershwin
Ira Gershwin
Lee Strasberg

19 WOODLAWN CEMETERY
Woodlawn, Bronx
Edward Kennedy "Duke" Ellington
Herman Melville
Joseph Pulitzer

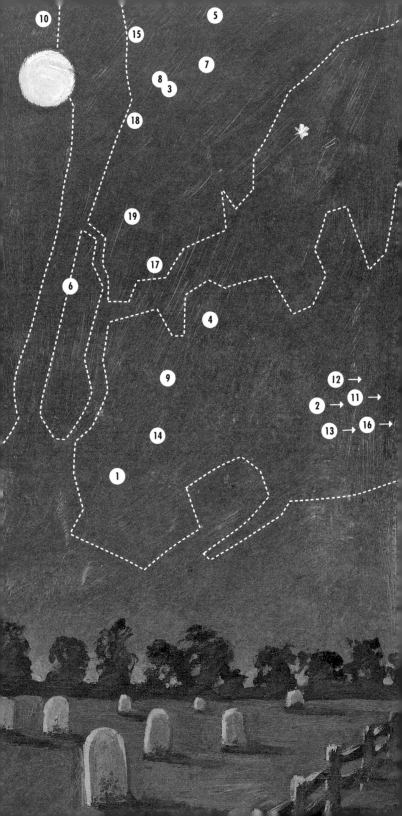

14 ORDERING IN

Kick off your shoes—you're home to stay. Now New York can come to you. Following are the city's best restaurants and markets that deliver (some charge extra; ask ahead) and various other businesses that make house calls.

In New York, most neighborhood liquor stores, Chinese restaurants, and pharmacies deliver. Most video stores provide pick-up and delivery service for members as do many dry cleaners.

BABYSITTING

1 Barnard College Babysitting Service
854-2035
M-F, 10am-5pm

BEAUTY

2 Christiana & Carmen
757-5811
Pedicure, manicure, massage.

COMPUTERS TO GO

3 PC Express Rentals
807-8234
24-hour rentals of computers and printers.

DOG WALKING

4 Pet Care Network, Inc.
889-0756, 545-0627
Private in-home care for dogs and dog walking.

EMERGENCIES

Electricians

5 Allen Electrical Services
254-9600

6 Michael Altman
681-2900

Exterminators

7 DNL Exterminating Co.
(718) 359-0646

Locksmith

8 Night & Day Locksmith
722-1017

Plumber

9 Brill & Brill Inc.
535-3210

Towing

10 AAA Road Service
757-3356

11 Jimmy's Towing
489-6718

EMPLOYMENT

12 CASH/Student Employment
998-4433
M-F, 9am-5pm
Hire students as bartenders, tutors, housesitters, for odd jobs.

HOUSEKEEPING

13 Danny Boy Cleaning Service
874-6130

14 Dirtbusters of Closets & Spaces/The Homemaker Service
721-4357

15 Lynn Agency
874-6130
Full service agency, baby nurses, butlers, chauffeurs, cooks, companions, house-keepers.

LIQUOR

16 Sherry-Lehmann
838-7500
M-Sat, 9am-7pm

MEDICAL SERVICES

17 Doctors on call
(718) 238-2100

18 New York Medical Housecalls
652-5858

NEWSPAPER DELIVERY

19 Lenox Hill Newspaper Delivery
879-1822

OVERNIGHT MAIL

20 Federal Express
(800) 238-5355
Delivery guaranteed to major U.S. cities by 10:30am the next morning. Messengers will pick up until 9:30pm.

21 UPS
695-7500
M-F, 8am-9pm
Delivery guaranteed by noon next day.

PERSONAL SERVICES

22 Lend A Hand
362-8200
All types of helpers: cooks, catering, babysitting, etc.

23 Red Tape Cutters
406-9898
Will do anything you don't want to: from picking up and delivering your tickets to renewing your passport—even wait at your home for a repairman!

PETS

24 Carol Wilbourn
741-0397
M-Sat, 9am- 6pm
Cat Therapist.

PHARMACY

25 Newton Pharmacy
838-6450

RENTING A FAX MACHINE

26 TTI Business Systems
679-3909

RESTAURANTS

27 Dial-A-Dinner: 779-1222
Daily, 3pm-10pm

Offers menus and delivery from the following restaurants:

*Akbar
Bistro at Trump Tower
Campagnola
Chin Chin
John Clancy's
La Côte Basque
Le Refuge
Marylou's
Old Homestead
Pen & Pencil
Petrossian Paris
Pietro's
Positano
Prunelle
Rusty Staub's on Fifth
Table d'Hôte
Via Via*

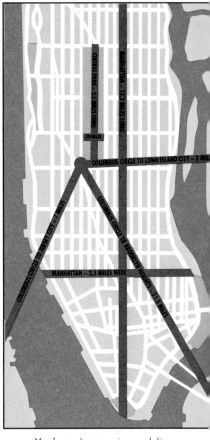

Manhattan's proportions and distances (as the crow flies.)
•

SPECIALTY STORES AND MARKETS

28 Balducci's
673-2600

29 Caviarteria
759-7410
(800) 4-CAVIAR

30 Dean & DeLuca
431-1691

31 Grace's Market Place
737-0600

32 Jefferson Market
675-2277

RUSSIAN NEW YORK

New York has been called 'Moscow on the Hudson,' a reference to the rich patterns and rhythm of life here, the city's kaleidoscope of changing scenes and its cultural variety. This was Moscow at the turn of the century, when Imperial Russia was still the force behind the city.

There is plenty of traditional Russian culture in New York, but almost everything we do here—even just buying ice cream on the street—was typical of life in Czarist Moscow.

PETER SCHAFFER, *Co-owner,* A La Vieille Russie

1 Intourist USSR
   630 Fifth Ave. at 52nd St.
   757-3884
   Agency for foreign travel.

2 New York Public Library
   Central Research Branch
   Fifth Ave. at 42nd St.
   Room 217
   930-0714
   Slavic and Baltic division.

3 Novoye Ruskoye Slova
   519 Eighth Ave.
   564-8544
   The oldest Russian daily in New York and the United States.

4 Russian National Bookstore
   321 East 14th St.
   475-1717

5 Russian Nobility Association
   of America
   971 First Ave.
   755-7528
   Keeper of the flame!

6 Russian Travel Bureau, Inc.
   225 East 44th St.
   986-1500
   Private tour company (since 1969).

7 Russian Voice
   130 East 16th St.
   475-7595
   The official weekly, advertisements in Russian and English.

8 Russica Book & Art Shop, Inc.
   799 Broadway at 11th St.
   Suite 301
   473-4780
   Russian language books, non-Soviet publications. Some gift and art items, prints, etc.

9 Soviet Import Export, Inc.
   460 West 34th St.
   947-8585
   Official trade agency.

10 Victor Kamkin, Inc.
   149 Fifth Ave. at 21st St.
   673-0776
   Russian language books, some in English, and many with side-by-side translations in several languages. All printed in the USSR Soviet gift items and souvenirs: Matrioshka dolls, lacquer boxes, records, tapes, sheet music, etc.

11 USSR Mission to the United
   Nations
   136 East 67th St.
   861-4900

RESTAURANTS

12 Caviarteria
   29 East 60th St.
   759-7410

13 Kalinka
   1067 Madison Ave. at 80th St.
   472-9656

14 Petrossian
   182 West 58th St.
   245-2214 (restaurant)
   245-2217 (food shop)
   Not for Russian ambiance, but for its reputation as the premier supplier of caviar.

15 Rasputin
   371 West 46th St.
   586-1860

16 Russian Samovar
   256 West 52nd St.
   757-0186

17 The Russian Tea Room
   150 West 57th St.
   265-0947
   (Also see *Russian Tea Room,* map #16.)

18 Troika
   148 West 67th St.
   724-0709

THE RUSSIAN TEA ROOM

What the 1990s are all about: movers and shakers dressing up, dressing down; people watching; just having fun.

RICHARD BARON, *Mâitre d'hôtel,* The Russian Tea Room

THE RUSSIAN TEA ROOM
150 West 57th St.
For reservations and information call 265-0947.

1 Susan Braudy, Vice President, Mercury/Douglas Films

2 Susan Blond, Music Business Publicist

3 Joe Armstrong, former Publisher, *New York* and *The Movies*;
Peter Minichiello, President, George Trescher Associates (Public Relations firm)

4 Jean Dalrymple, Theatrical Producer

5 Johnnie Planco, William Morris Agent

6 Lynn Nesbit, Superagent
Susan Gluck, ICM Agent
Helen Verno, Senior Vice President, Creative Affairs, Highgate Pictures

7 Linda Janklow, married to Literary Agent Morton Janklow

8 Roberta Ashley, Executive Editor, *Cosmopolitan*

9 Sally Lefkowitz, widow of the late William Morris agent, Nat Lefkowitz

10 Garson Kanin
Michael Caine
Woody Allen

11 Gerald Schoenfeld, Shubert Theater Mogul
Diane Sawyer, TV News Star
Mike Nichols, Broadway and Movie Director

12 Melanie Griffith;
Don Johnson

13 Sam Cohn, ICM Legend
Robert Benton, Director
Arthur Penn, Director
Peter Yates, Director

14 Sigourney Weaver
Alan King, Comic
Richard Gere
Cindy Crawford

15 Robert Lantz, Literary Agent

16 Noel Behn, Author

17 Bobby Zarem, Supertalented Publicist

18 Boaty Boatwright, William Morris Agent
Steve Starr, William Morris Agent

19 A.E. Hotchner, Author

20 Judy Gordon, Theatrical Producer

21 Lois Smith, Publicist

22 Barry Landau, Superflack

23 Andrew Bergman, Screenwriter
Joel Siegel, TV Critic
Michael Kramer, *U.S. News* writer
Jerry Della Femina, Adman
Jeff Greenfield, *ABC News* correspondent
Gerry Imber, Plastic Surgeon to the Stars

24 Jim Stein, William Morris Rising Star

25 Diane Sokolow, Film Producer

NOTE: This map does not represent the Russian Tea Room's table numbering plan.

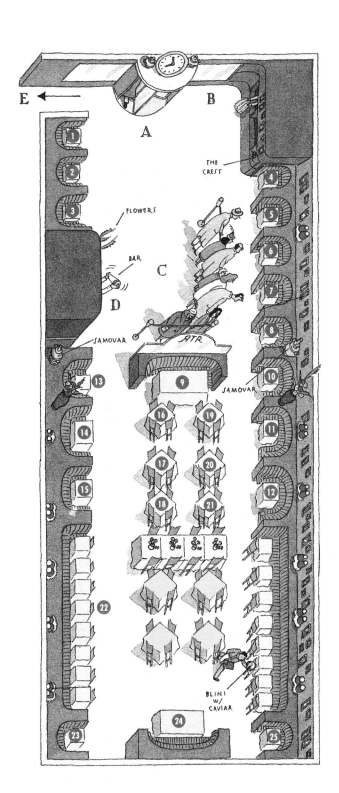

BUSINESS TOKYO'S EAST MEETS WEST

For a week or so each spring, the cherry blossoms at Grant's Tomb and parts of Central Park bring back thoughts of Japan. In 1910, the then First Lady, Mrs. William Howard Taft, nudged the mayor of Tokyo into giving saplings to New York and Washington. For more than eighty years, a rich burst of springtime color has reminded New Yorkers of their sister city on the other side of the world.

ANTHONY PAUL, *Editor-in-Chief*, Business Tokyo *magazine*

ART AND CULTURE

1 Asia Society
725 Park Ave.
288-6400

2 Cherry Blossoms—Grant's Tomb
Riverside Dr. at 122nd St.
666-1640

3 Consulate General of Japan
299 Park Ave.
371-8222

4 Japan Society
333 East 47th St.
832-1155
Lectures, films, instruction.

5 Kokushi Budo Institute of New York
331 Riverside Dr.
866-6777
Judo, jujitsu, karate instruction.

6 The Nippon Club
115 East 57th St.
753-9090
Business club; members and guests only.

7 Ronin Gallery
605 Madison Ave.
688-0188
Japanese prints.

8 Statue of Shinran
Riverside Dr. at 105th St.
Founder of Buddhist sect.

9 Tokyo Video
7 West 44th St.
921-1449

BOOKSTORES

10 Books Nippon
115 West 57th St.
582-4622
Specializes in art books.

11 Kinokuniya
10 West 49th St.
765-1461

FOR THE HOME

12 Azuma
25 East 8th St.
673-2900
Tatami mats.

13 Katagiri & Co.
224 East 59th St.
755-3566
Household products and groceries.

14 Kimono House
120 Thompson St.
966-5936
Large selection of kimonos.

15 Koyo International
39 West 46th St.
575-0233
Chinaware.

16 Maxima USA, Inc.
575 Fifth Ave.
355-2545
Department store that caters to Japanese tourists.

17 Miya Shoji and Interiors, Inc.
109 West 17th St.
243-6774
Shoji, traditional paper screens.

18 Sam Bok Grocery Store
127 West 43rd St.
582-4730
Korean store where one can buy many Japanese food products.

19 Things Japanese
1109 Lexington Ave. bet. 77th and 78th Sts.
249-3591
Household goods.

20 Tsumura International Inc.
400 Madison Ave.
421-4490
Traditional Japanese bath products, including Basu Kurin salts.

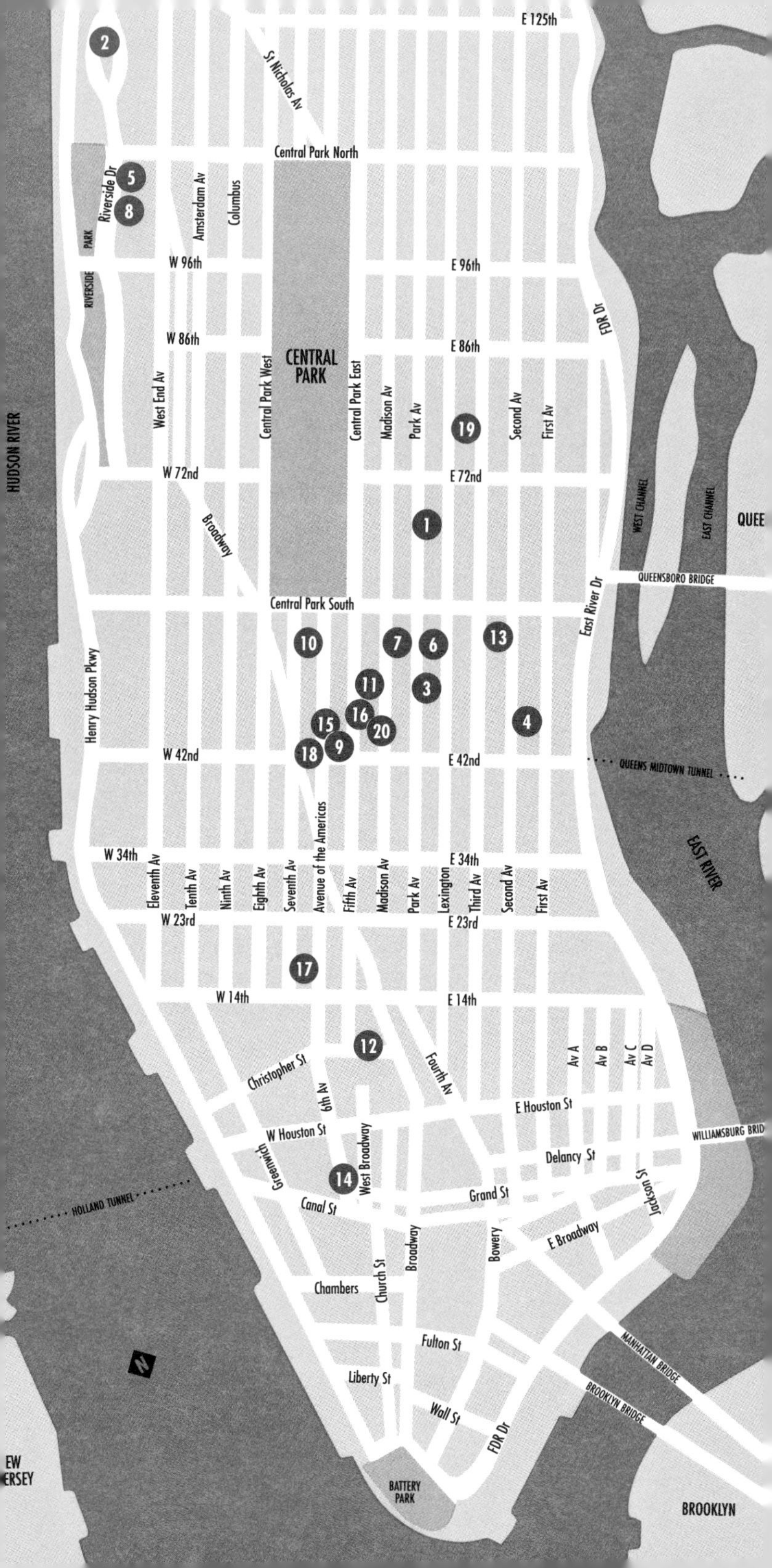

E 125th
St Nicholas Av
Central Park North
Riverside Dr
Amsterdam Av
Columbus
PARK
RIVERSIDE
W 96th
E 96th
W 86th
E 86th
CENTRAL PARK
FDR Dr
West End Av
Central Park West
Central Park East
Madison Av
Park Av
Second Av
First Av
HUDSON RIVER
W 72nd
E 72nd
Broadway
WEST CHANNEL
EAST CHANNEL
QUEE
QUEENSBORO BRIDGE
East River Dr
Central Park South
Henry Hudson Pkwy
W 42nd
E 42nd
QUEENS MIDTOWN TUNNEL
EAST RIVER
W 34th
E 34th
Eleventh Av
Tenth Av
Ninth Av
Eighth Av
Seventh Av
Avenue of the Americas
Fifth Av
Madison Av
Park Av
Lexington
Third Av
Second Av
First Av
W 23rd
E 23rd
W 14th
E 14th
Christopher St
Fourth Av
Av A
Av B
Av C
Av D
6th Av
E Houston St
W Houston St
WILLIAMSBURG BRID
Greenwich
West Broadway
Delancy St
Jackson St
HOLLAND TUNNEL
Canal St
Grand St
E Broadway
Church St
Broadway
Bowery
Chambers
Fulton St
MANHATTAN BRIDGE
Liberty St
BROOKLYN BRIDGE
Wall St
FDR Dr
EW
ERSEY
BATTERY PARK
BROOKLYN
1
2
3
4
5
6
7
8
9
10
11
12
13
14
15
16
17
18
19
20

BUSINESS TOKYO'S TASTES OF JAPAN

RESTAURANTS

1 Chibo
47 East 44th St.
297-0199
Best okonomiyaki, traditional food from Osaka and Hiroshima.

2 46th St. Strip bet. Fifth and Sixth Aves.
Yakitori restaurants and karaoke bars.

3 Hatsuhana
17 East 48th St.
355-3345
Fine sushi, among NY's best.

4 Ichiban 39
45 West 39th St.
382-2296
Delicatessen.

5 Inagiku
111 East 49th St.
355-0440
At the Waldorf.

6 Japonica
90 University Pl.
243-7752
Cozy, neighborhood place.

7 Kurumazushi
18 West 56th St.
541-9030
Pricey, mainly sushi and sashimi.

8 Mitsukoshi
461 Park Ave.
935-6444
Great quality, varied menu, Park Avenue prices.

9 Mugi
132 West 58th St.
757-5842
Real Japanese food, not altered to suit American taste.

10 New York Hilton
53rd Street at Sixth Ave.
586-7000
Traditional Japanese breakfast.

11 Nippon Restaurant
155 East 52nd St.
688-5941
For midtown connoisseurs.

12 Omen Restaurant
113 Thompson St.
966-8923
Best udon, thick noodles.

13 The Quilted Giraffe
550 Madison Ave.
593-1221
Serves kaiseki, traditional 10-course Japanese meal.

14 Sapporo
152 West 49th St.
869-8972
Inexpensive for lunch.

15 Seryna
11 East 53rd St.
980-9393
Steaks cooked on hot stones.

16 Sushisay
38 East 51st St.
755-1780
Sushi only. Trendy; frequented by famous Japanese columnist, and often written up in Tokyo newspapers.

TRADITIONAL NOODLE SHOPS

17 Daiichi Kosho
353 West 48th St.
586-6200

18 Hakata
230 West 48th St.
245-1020

19 Shinwa
Olympic Tower
645 Fifth Ave
644-7400

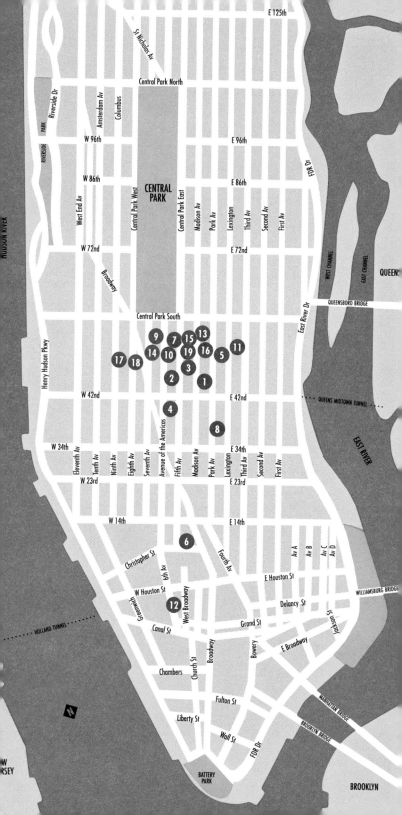

THOMAS HOVING'S TREASURES OF THE METROPOLITAN MUSEUM OF ART

The Metropolitan Museum of Art
Fifth Ave. at 82nd St.
General information:
535-7710

The Cloisters Branch
Fort Tryon Park
923-3700

2

**Second
Floor**

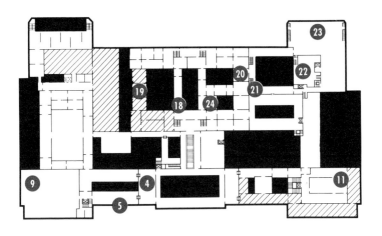

1

**First
Floor**

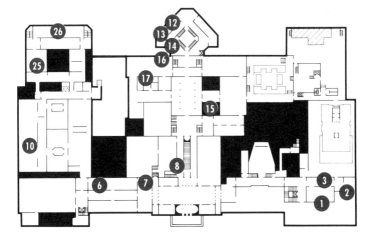

HIGH TEA

To be invited to tea at an English household usually implies just a cup of tea and biscuits. High Tea at a hotel or restaurant in New York, however, is a much fancier affair. Served between 3 and 6pm, it may include an assortment of dainty sandwiches—egg, cucumber, smoked salmon, and watercress—followed by scones, jam, and cream, small French pastries or layer cake.

JOAN BROWN, *British Nanny in New York*

1 The Algonquin
59 West 44th St.
The Lobby
840-6800

2 Berkshire Place
21 East 52nd St.
The Atrium
753-5800

3 The Carlyle
Madison Ave. at East 76th St.
The Red Room
744-1600

4 Helmsley Palace
455 Madison Ave.
The Gold Room
888-7000

5 Le Train Bleu at
Bloomingdale's
1000 Third Ave. at 59th St.
Dining room
705-2000

6 Little Nell's Tea Room
345 East 85th St.
Dining rooms
772-2046

7 The Lowell Hotel
28 East 63rd St.
The Pembroke Room
838-1400

8 Mayfair Regent
610 Park Ave.
Tea is served off the lobby
288-0800

9 Peninsula Hotel
700 Fifth Ave.
The Gotham Lounge
247-2200

10 The Pierre
2 East 61st St. at Fifth Ave.
The Rotunda Room
838-8000

11 The Plaza Hotel
Fifth Ave. at 59th St.
The Palm Court
759-3000

12 Sant Ambroeus
1000 Madison Ave. at 77th St.
570-2211

13 Sarabeth's Kitchen
Dining room
423 Amsterdam Ave.
496-6280

14 1295 Madison Ave.
410-7335

15 The Stanhope
995 Fifth Ave.
The Salon
288-5800

16 Waldorf-Astoria Hotel
301 Park Ave. at East 50th St.
The Cocktail Terrace
355-3000

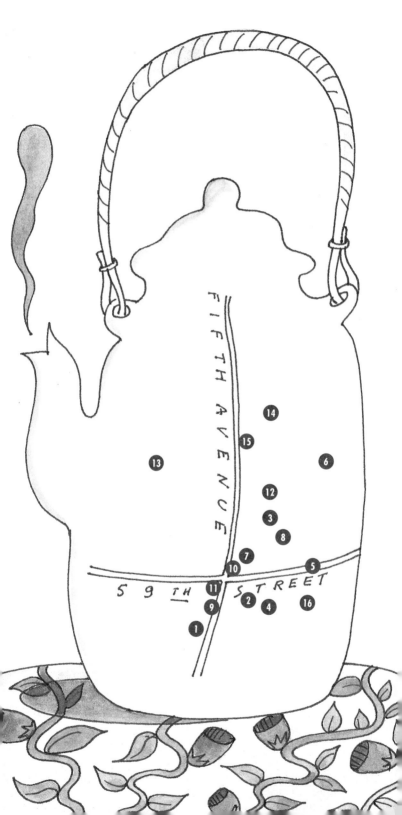

1 Balducci's
424 Sixth Ave.
673-2600
M-Sat, 7am-8:30pm;
Sun, 7am-6:30pm

2 D & G Bakery
45 Spring St.
226-6688
Daily, 8am-2pm

3 E.A.T.
1064 Madison Ave.
772-0022
Daily, 8am-10pm

4 Ecce Panis
1120 Third Ave.
535-2099
M-F, 10am-7pm;
Sat-Sun, 10am-6pm

5 Gertel's Bakery
53 Hester St.
982-3250
M-Th, Sun, 7am-5pm;
F, 7am,-2pm

6 H & H Bagels
2239 Broadway
595-8000

7 Kossar's Bialy Bakery
367 Grand St.
473-4810
Daily, 24 hours

8 Moishe's Bakery
181 East Houston St.
475-9624
M-Th, Sun, 7am-6pm;
F, 7am-4pm

9 Orwasher's Bakery
308 East 78th St.
288-6569
M-Sat, 7am-7pm

10 Palermo Bakery
213 First Ave.
254-4139
M-Sat, 7am-7pm;
Sun, 7am-2pm

11 Trio French Bakery
476 Ninth Ave.
695-4296
M-F, 5:30am-3pm

12 Zito's Bakery
259 Bleecker St.
929-6139
M-Sat, 6am-6pm;
Sun, 6am-12pm

13 Zabar's
2245 Broadway
787-2000
Mon-F, 8am-7:30pm;
Sat, 8am-midnight;
Sun, 9am-6pm

BEST CHEESE

1 Alleva Dairy
188 Grand St.
226-7990
M-Sat, 8:30am-6pm;
Sun, 8:30am-2pm

2 Balducci's
424 Sixth Ave.
673-2600
Daily, 7am-8:30pm.

3 Ben's Cheese Shop
181 East Houston St.
254-8290
M-F, 8:30am-5:30pm;
Sun, 7:45am-5:30pm

4 Cheese of All Nations
153 Chambers St.
732-0752
M-Sat, 8am-5:30pm

5 Dean & DeLuca
560 Broadway
431-1691
M-Sat, 8am-8pm;
Sun, 9am-7pm

6 Di Luca Dairy and Deli
484 Ninth Ave.
563-2774
Tue-Sat, 9am-6:30pm

7 East Village Cheese
34 Third Ave.
477-2601
M-F, 9am-6:30pm;
Sat-Sun, 6:30am-5:30pm

8 Fairway
2127 Broadway
595-1888
M-F, 8am-midnight;
Sat-Sun, 8am-10pm

9 Grace's Market Place
1237 Third Ave.
737-0600
M-Sat, 7am-8:30pm;
Sun, 8am-7:30pm

10 Ideal Cheese Shop
1205 Second Ave.
688-7579
M-F, 9am-6:30pm;
Sat, 9am-6pm

11 Joe's Dairy
156 Sullivan St.
677-8780
Tue-Sat, 7am-6:30pm;
Sun, 9am-12:30pm

12 Murray's Cheese
42 Cornelia St.
243-3289
M-Sat, 8:30am-6pm

13 Todaro Brothers
555 Second Ave.
532-0633
M-Sat, 7:30am-9pm;
Sun, 8am-8pm

14 Zabar's
2245 Broadway
787-2000
M-F, 8am-7:30pm;
Sat, 8am-midnight;
Sun, 9am-6pm

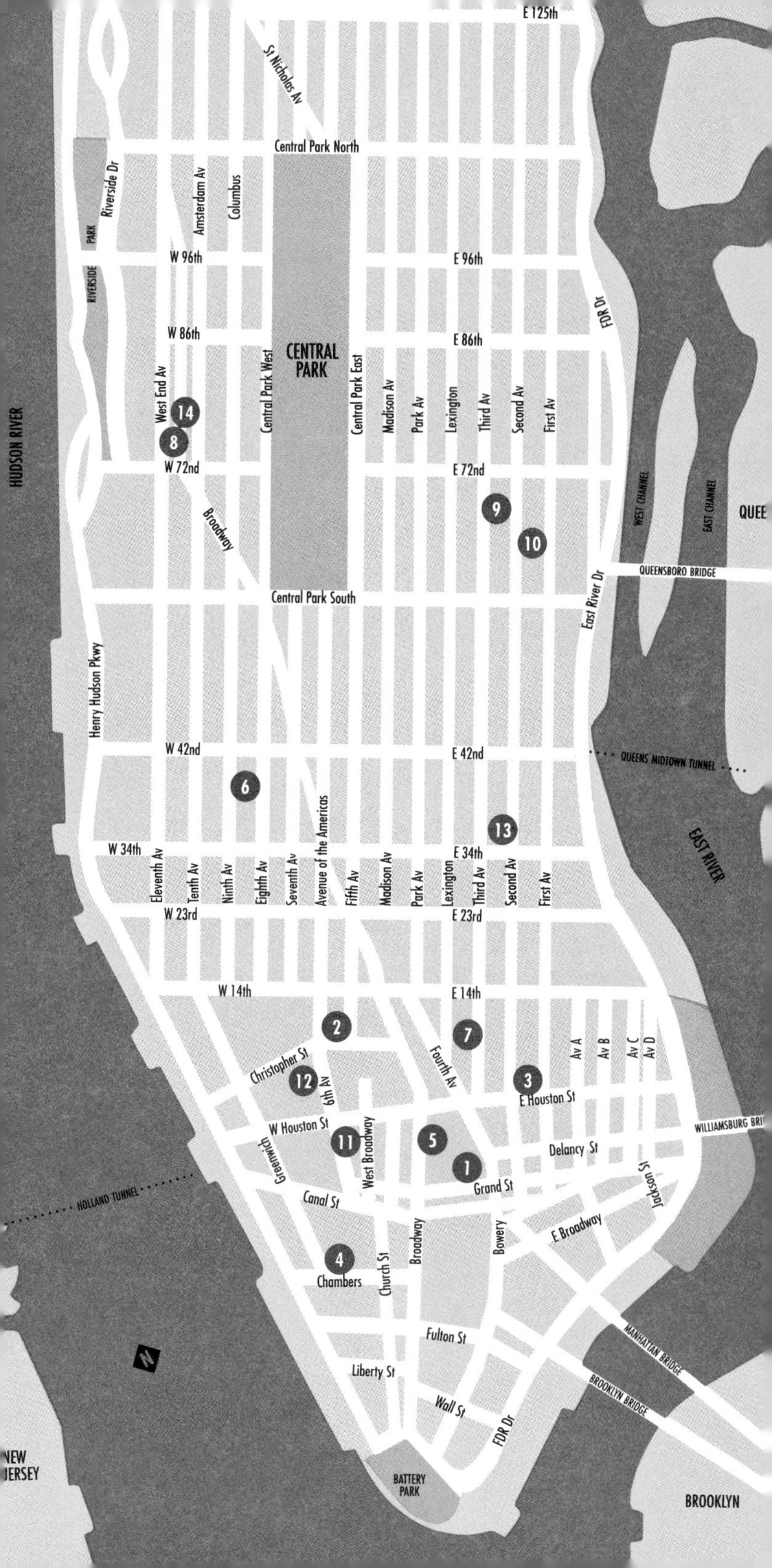
E 125th
St Nicholas Av
Central Park North
Riverside Dr
PARK
RIVERSIDE
Amsterdam Av
Columbus
W 96th
E 96th
FDR Dr
W 86th
E 86th
CENTRAL PARK
West End Av
Central Park West
Central Park East
Madison Av
Park Av
Lexington
Third Av
Second Av
First Av
HUDSON RIVER
W 72nd
E 72nd
Broadway
WEST CHANNEL
EAST CHANNEL
QUEE
QUEENSBORO BRIDGE
Central Park South
East River Dr
Henry Hudson Pkwy
W 42nd
E 42nd
QUEENS MIDTOWN TUNNEL
EAST RIVER
W 34th
E 34th
Eleventh Av
Tenth Av
Ninth Av
Eighth Av
Seventh Av
Avenue of the Americas
Fifth Av
Madison Av
Park Av
Lexington
Third Av
Second Av
First Av
W 23rd
E 23rd
W 14th
E 14th
Fourth Av
Av A
Av B
Av C
Av D
Christopher St
6th Av
E Houston St
W Houston St
West Broadway
WILLIAMSBURG BRI
Delancy St
Greenwich
Grand St
Jackson St
HOLLAND TUNNEL
Canal St
Bowery
E Broadway
Church St
Broadway
Chambers
MANHATTAN BRIDGE
Fulton St
Liberty St
BROOKLYN BRIDGE
Wall St
FDR Dr
NEW JERSEY
BATTERY PARK
BROOKLYN
1
2
3
4
5
6
7
8
9
10
11
12
13
14

23 URBAN OASES

Nestled amongst New York's cold, hard-edged skyscrapers, pockets of green give life to the concrete jungle. Small gardens thrive in corporate lobbies, courtyards, and between buildings—places of calm in the maelstrom of the city.

1 AT & T
550 Madison bet. 55th and 56th Sts.

2 Biblical Garden
The Cathedral of St. John the Divine
Amsterdam Ave. at 112th St.
Only plants mentioned in the Bible are grown here.

3 Crystal Pavillion
Third Ave. at 50th St.
Waterfalls.

4 Equitable Center
787 Seventh Ave. bet. 51st and 52nd Sts.
Branch of the Whitney Museum.

5 Ford Foundation
320 East 43rd St.
Ten-story tropical hothouse with skylight.

6 General Theological Seminary
135 Ninth Avenue
M-F, 12pm-3pm;
Sat, 11am-4pm;
Sun, 2pm-4pm

7 IBM Garden Plaza
590 Madison Ave. at 56th St.
IBM Gallery of Art.

8 Isamu Noguchi Garden Museum
32-27 Vernon Ave., Long Island City
Open April-November,
W and Sat, 11am-6pm
A garden for meditation in the Japanese manner.

9 Jefferson Library Rose Garden
425 Sixth Ave. at 8th St.
Sat-Sun, 1pm-5pm
Lovely for strolling.

10 Park Ave. Plaza
55 East 52nd St.
Waterfall.

11 Philip Morris Sculpture Court
120 Park Ave. at 42nd St.
Branch of the Whitney Museum; musical performances.

12 Rockefeller Center
630 Fifth Ave. bet. 49th and 50th Sts.
Fountains and seasonal plantings; musical performances.

13 Shakespeare Garden
South of Delacorte Theater in Central Park near West 80th St.
Seeds and cuttings from Shakespeare's garden in Stratford-on-Avon.

14 St. John's Episcopal Church
224 Waverly Place at West 11th St.
Church office entrance to garden.

15 St. Luke in the Fields Church
487 Hudson St. bet. Christopher and Grove Sts.
A dreamy English garden.

16 World Financial Center
Intersection of West, Church, Vesey and Liberty Sts.
Hudson River views.

17 United Nations
405 East 42nd St.
Rose bushes, cherry blossoms overlooking East River.

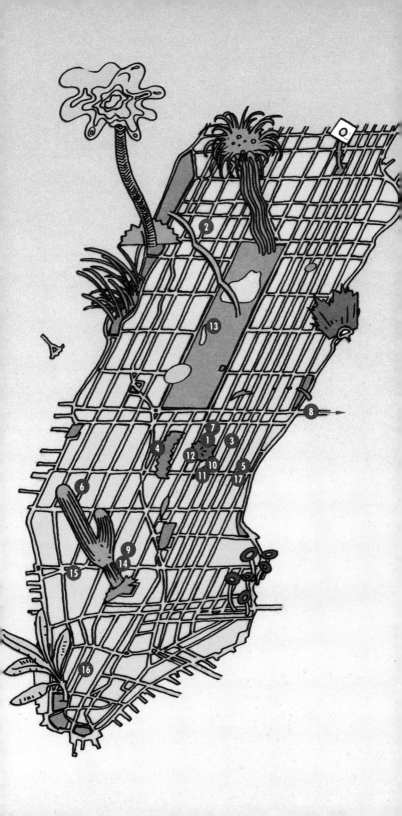

24

12 ITALIAN RESTAURANTS
(A Master Chef's Choice)

We Italians are very sensual. As a chef and restaurant owner, food is my obsession; the aromas, the textures, the colors, and the flavors of nature's bounty are my palette.

I am crazy about living in New York. This town offers endless possibilities for experiencing every type of cooking imaginable. The following restaurants offer some of my favorite Italian food in the city.

FRANCESCO ANTONUCCI, *Executive Chef, Remi, New York, Los Angeles*

1 Bice
7 East 54th St.
688-1999
Fun for lunch—and people watching each other in mirrors.

2 Bistro
Trump Tower
725 Fifth Ave.
832-1555
The spot for sandwich and espresso when you are on Fifth Avenue.

3 Elio's
1621 Second Ave.
772-2242
Casual Italian with a great atmosphere.

4 Erminia
250 East 83rd St.
879-4284
If you want the feeling of a chalet in Cortina d'Ampezzo.

5 Felidia
243 East 58 St.
758-1479
For a wonderful Italian wine selection.

6 Grotta Azzurra
387 Broome St.
925-8775
The most alive Trattoria in Little Italy.

7 Malvasia
108 East 60th St.
223-4790
The only place I eat pasta in town.

8 Mezzaluna
1295 Third Ave. bet. 74th and 75th Sts.
535-9600
Best pizza in New York; Aldo is the most authentic restaurateur in town.

9 Mezzogiorno
195 Spring St.
334-2112
Mezzaluna's larger downtown sister with terrific pasta and pizza.

10 Palio
Equitable Center
151 West 54 St.
245-4850

11 San Domenico
240 Central Park South
265-5959
As a restaurateur I often take my assistant chef to show off the food presentations here and at Palio.

12 Sant Ambroeus
1000 Madison Ave. at 77th St.
570-2211
Standing at the bar sipping a cappuccino it feels just like Milan.

25

A DOZEN ROMANTIC SETTINGS

As a transplanted Parisian I feel Paris is the epitome of romance. New York is modern and hard; it seems built with only money in mind.

Here it is a challenge to create romance. One has to invent or imagine it. Yet what a thrill it is when one finds it—on a cobblestone street, lined with trees and charming old houses, or on the deck of the Staten Island Ferry at dusk.

HERVÉ AARON, *President*, Didier Aaron Inc., *New York*

1. Boating on the lake in Central Park
   Near West 72nd St. entrance
   517-2233

2. Dinosaur Gallery in the American Museum of Natural History
   Central Park West at 79th St.
   769-5100

3. Flea Market, Sixth Ave. at 26th St.
   Weekends only.

4. Frick Courtyard
   1 East 70th St.
   288-0700

5. Former office of Mr. Morgan
   Pierpont Morgan Library
   29 East 36th St.
   685-0610

6. Four Seasons Grill (for dinner)
   99 East 52nd St.
   754-9494

7. The Herb Garden and Trie Cloisters at The Cloisters
   Fort Tryon Park
   923-3700

8. Observation deck of Rockefeller Center
   630 Fifth Ave.
   65th Floor
   632-5000

9. The Palm Court (for lunch)
   The Plaza Hotel
   768 Fifth Ave.
   546-5350

10. Staten Island Ferry
    Foot of Whitehall St. at Battery Park
    727-2508
    Round trip for 25 cents.

11. Strolling along Wall Street on Sunday

12. The Temple of Dendur
    The Metropolitan Museum of Art
    Fifth Ave. at 82nd St.
    535-7710

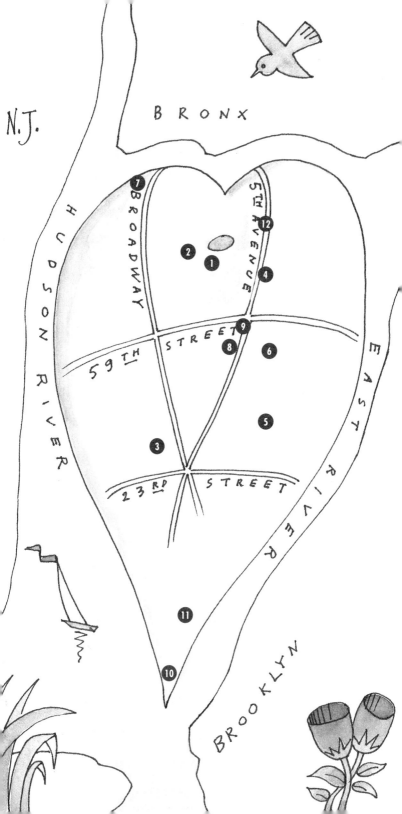

26

ROTTEN NEW YORK I
(Scandals)

Is the Big Apple Rotten? Not on your life. It isn't possible to be a hero without a good villain and New York has a way of producing the best of both.

BILL HARRIS, *New York History Writer*

1 1906: The girl on the red velvet swing
Madison Ave. at 26th St.
Architect Stanford White shot by Harry K. Thaw in what was at that time Madison Square Garden.

2 1929: Love Nest
29 West 81st St. bet. Central Park West and Columbus Ave.
Real estate millionaire Edward "Daddy" Browning sets up housekeeping with his fifteen-year-old bride, the former Frances "Peaches" Heenan.

3 1930: Where Is Judge Crater?
West 45th St. bet. Eighth and Ninth Aves.
State Supreme Court Justice Joseph Force Crater vanishes forever.

4 1932: Beau James
6 St. Luke's Pl.
Mayor James J. Walker resigns as Mayor rather than face trial for corruption.

5 1935: God's kingdom
152 West 126th St.
Father Divine, a.k.a. "God," leads thousands to salvation in a baby blue Rolls Royce.

6 1978: Chelsea Hotel
222 West 23rd St.
Sid Vicious purportedly knifed Nancy Spungen in Room 100. Room 100 no longer exists.

7 1970: Holdout
Five buildings at the SE corner of Third Ave. and 53rd St., surrounded by 875 Third Ave.
Rent-controlled tenants get drug abusers and prostitutes as neighbors thanks to a developer who can't think of any other way to get rid of them. They still refuse to move, and get a skyscraper for a neighbor.

8 1979: "The Office"
13 West 54th St., just west of Fifth Ave.
Former governor Nelson Rockefeller dies of a heart attack in his townhouse while working with his assistant, Megan Marshak, who waits an hour before reporting it.

9 1980: The Dakota
1 West 72nd St., corner of Central Park West
Ex-Beatle John Lennon shot dead.

10 1984: Mayflower Madam
304 West 74th St. bet. Broadway and West End Ave.
Sydney Biddle Barrows arrested for running a call girl operation.

11 1987: New York County Courthouse
East side of Foley Square at Worth St.
Bess Meyerson, a former Miss America and New York City official, charged with—then acquitted of—improperly influencing Judge Hortense Gable, who was handling the divorce case of her boyfriend, Andy Capasso.

12 1989: Park Lane Hotel
Central Park South bet. Fifth and Sixth Aves.)
Leona Helmsley, New York's Hotel Queen, is convicted of evading income taxes after having been quoted in her trial as saying, "Only little people pay taxes."

13 1990: Trump Tower
725 Fifth Ave.
Real estate developer and gambling entrepreneur Donald Trump tells his wife, Ivana, that their 13-year-marriage is coming to an end because he's found a younger love. Critics say it's a publicity stunt; Donald says, "It's good for business."

27

ROTTEN NEW YORK II
(Corruption)

1 1912: Arbor Dance Hall
Seventh Ave. at 52nd St.
*Owney "The Killer"
Madden, ambushed by eleven
thugs, is hit by a dozen bullets
and says, "It ain't nobody's
business but mine who put
these slugs in me." All eleven
would-be assassins are dead
before Owney leaves the hos-
pital.*

2 1920s: Jungle Alley
123rd St. bet. Lenox and
Seventh Aves.
*Harlem's biggest concentra-
tion of speakeasies and night-
clubs.*

3 1923: Coll Calling
23rd St. west of Seventh Ave.
*Vincent "Mad Dog" Coll
machine-gunned to death in a
phone booth.*

4 1927: Gotcha
103 Norfolk St. bet. Delancey
and Rivington Sts.
*Jake Orgen, a.k.a. Little
Augie, gunned down in front
of his bodyguard, Legs
Diamond.*

5 1928: Fairfield Apartments
20 West 72nd St. bet. Central
Park West and Columbus Ave.
*Gangster Arnold Rothstein
killed in an argument over a
poker game.*

6 1933: Ansonia Hotel
2109 Broadway at West
74th St.
*Bank robber and frequent
prison escapee, Willie "The
Actor" Sutton, arrested for his
all-time favorite heist, a bank
job at Broadway and 110th St.*

7 1933: Half Moon Cafe
Broadway at 80th St.
*Waxey Gordon rubs out Dutch
Schultz with a machine gun
from a passing car.*

8 1938-48: Passing the Buck
204 West 96th St., east of
Amsterdam Ave.
*Edward Mueller eludes trea-
sury agents for ten years passing thousands of homemade
imitation dollar bills with
misspelled words and engrav-
ings that seem to have been
cut with a steak knife and
becomes America's most successful counterfeiter.*

9 1957: Majestic Apartments
115 Central Park West bet.
71st and 72nd Sts.
*Francesco Castiglia, a.k.a.
Frank Costello, "The Prime
Minister of the Underworld,"
shot after singing on national
television, but survives to
move to the suburbs.*

10 1957: Park Central Hotel
Seventh Ave. at 55th St., NW
corner; now Omni Park
Hotel
*Labor racketeer Albert
Anastasia shot by persons
unknown while having a
haircut.*

11 1971: Columbus Circle
SW corner of Central Park
*Godfather Joe Columbo shot
in front of thousands of wit-
nesses while making a speech
at an Italian-American Day
Unity rally.*

12 1972: Umberto's Clam House
129 Mulberry St. at Hester St.
*Godfather-hopeful Joey Gallo
gunned down at his own
birthday party.*

28

INCOME BY ZIP CODE

According to *The Sourcebook of Demographics and Buying Power for Every ZIP Code in the USA,** nearly one quarter of the Upper East Side's 10022, 10021, 10028 and 10128 households have yearly incomes of more than $75,000. Almost half of all households in Clinton, East Harlem, and parts of Central Harlem and Morningside Heights make less than $10,000 per year.

AVERAGE YEARLY
INCOME BY ZIP
CODE (per household)

	ZIP	Income
1	10001	$27,662.
2	10002	$21,031.
3	10003	$34,666.
4	10004	$40,093.
5	10005	$44,444.
6	10006	$31,609.
7	10007	$28,358.
8	10009	$19,166.
9	10010	$39,386.
10	10011	$33,828.
11	10012	$31,107.
12	10013	$28,715.
13	10014	$33,290.
14	10016	$37,625.
15	10017	$43,297.
16	10018	$18,061.
17	10019	$30,935.
18	10020	$33,656.
19	10021	$46,210.
20	10022	$46,328.
21	10023	$38,100.
22	10024	$36,602.
23	10025	$30,085.
24	10026	$14,914.
25	10027	$22,592.
26	10028	$44,499.
27	10029	$22,234.
28	10035	$15,758.
29	10036	$20,992.
30	10038	$30,588.
31	10128	$42,869.

*© 1989 CACI, Sixth Edition, Second Printing

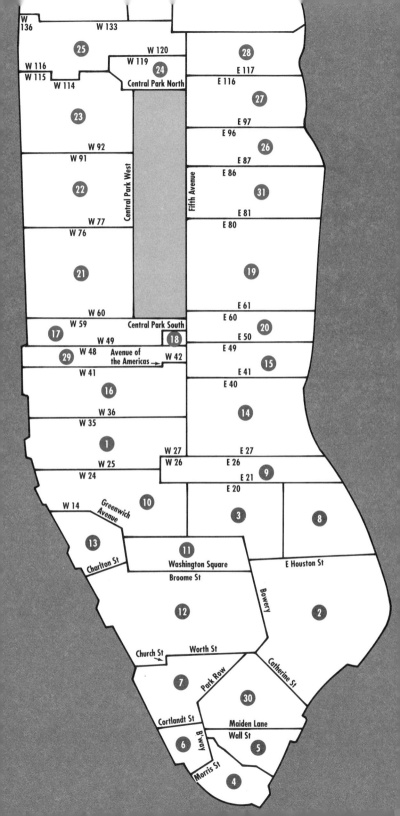

POOL HALLS

New York is one of the few places in the world where you can't get a beer in a pool room.   Which is why it costs so much ($10-12/hour) to play. The only products the room owner can sell are time and space.

The New York pool scene is a great dating scene. Billiard halls used to be the working guy's place to relax; now the clubs are full of couples.

BILLIE BILLING, *Pool Champion, Instructor*

1 21 Billiards
2121 Broadway
721-1909

2 The Amsterdam Billiard Club
344 Amsterdam Ave. bet.
76th and 77th Sts.
496-8180

3 The Billiard Club
220 West 19th St.
206-7665

4 Blatt Bowling & Billiard
Corporation
809 Broadway
674-8855
Equipment suppliers.

5 Chelsea Billiards
54 West 21st St.
989-0096

6 City Hall Billiards
31 Park Row
962-9210

7 Cue Club
88 Reade St.
571-6702

8 Jack's Billiards
614 Ninth Ave.
315-5225

9 Julian's Billiard Academy
138 East 14th St.
475-9334

10 Le Q
36 East 12th St.
995-8512

11 Society Billiards
10 East 21st St.
529-8600

12 Tekk Billiards
75 Christopher St.
463-9282

13 West Side Billiards
601 West 50th St.
246-1060

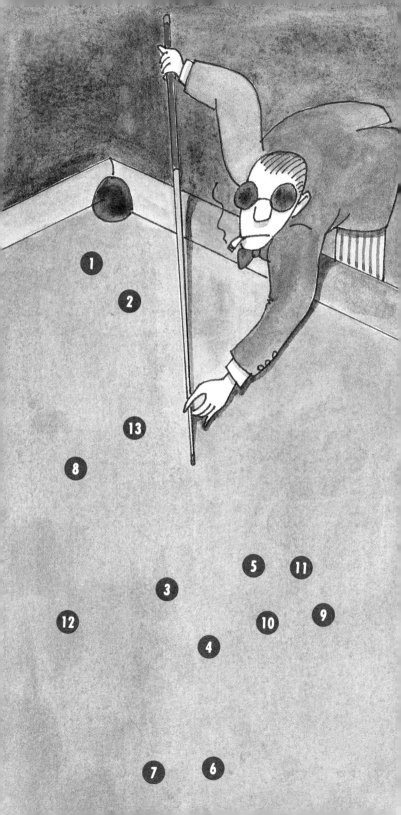

30

SUBWAYS

New York's subways are fast and cheap. And in a city where time is money and money is, well, money, the subway is the best deal around. For less than the cost of stepping into a cab, you can travel for 236 miles, unburdened by traffic or street lights, throughout Manhattan and its boroughs.

A massive network of tunnels, trains and buses, the New York City Transit Authority is an institution unto itself, employing the sixth largest police force in the nation and housing its own museum. Four billion dollars a year are spent operating and maintaining the city's subways and buses. Outrageous, perhaps, but consider this: it takes three million dollars to replace the vandalized train windows alone!

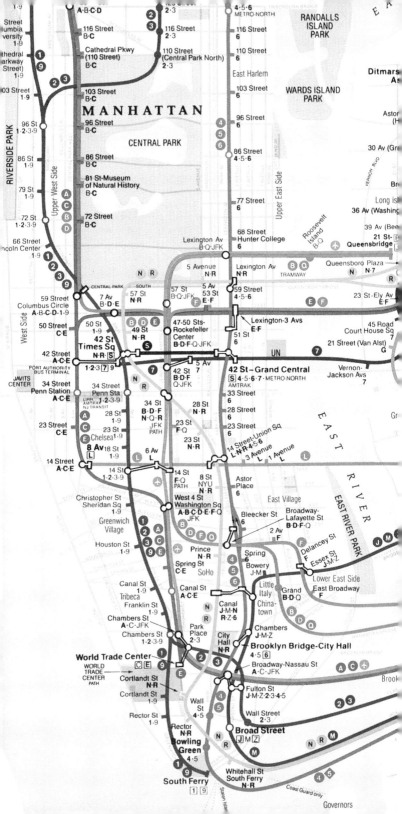

31 BUSES

These mastodons are practically the only public transit crosstown in the borough of Manhattan. Despite the fact that you need exact change in coins, the buses offer certain advantages to the speedier subway. There is plenty of time to view skyscrapers and street scenes from the oversize tinted windows. Also, most buses are air-conditioned, have wheelchair access and are equipped with that marvelous hydraulic mechanism that allows them to "kneel" in order to receive older passengers who can't step up; mighty considerate to the passenger who would have trouble using the subway.

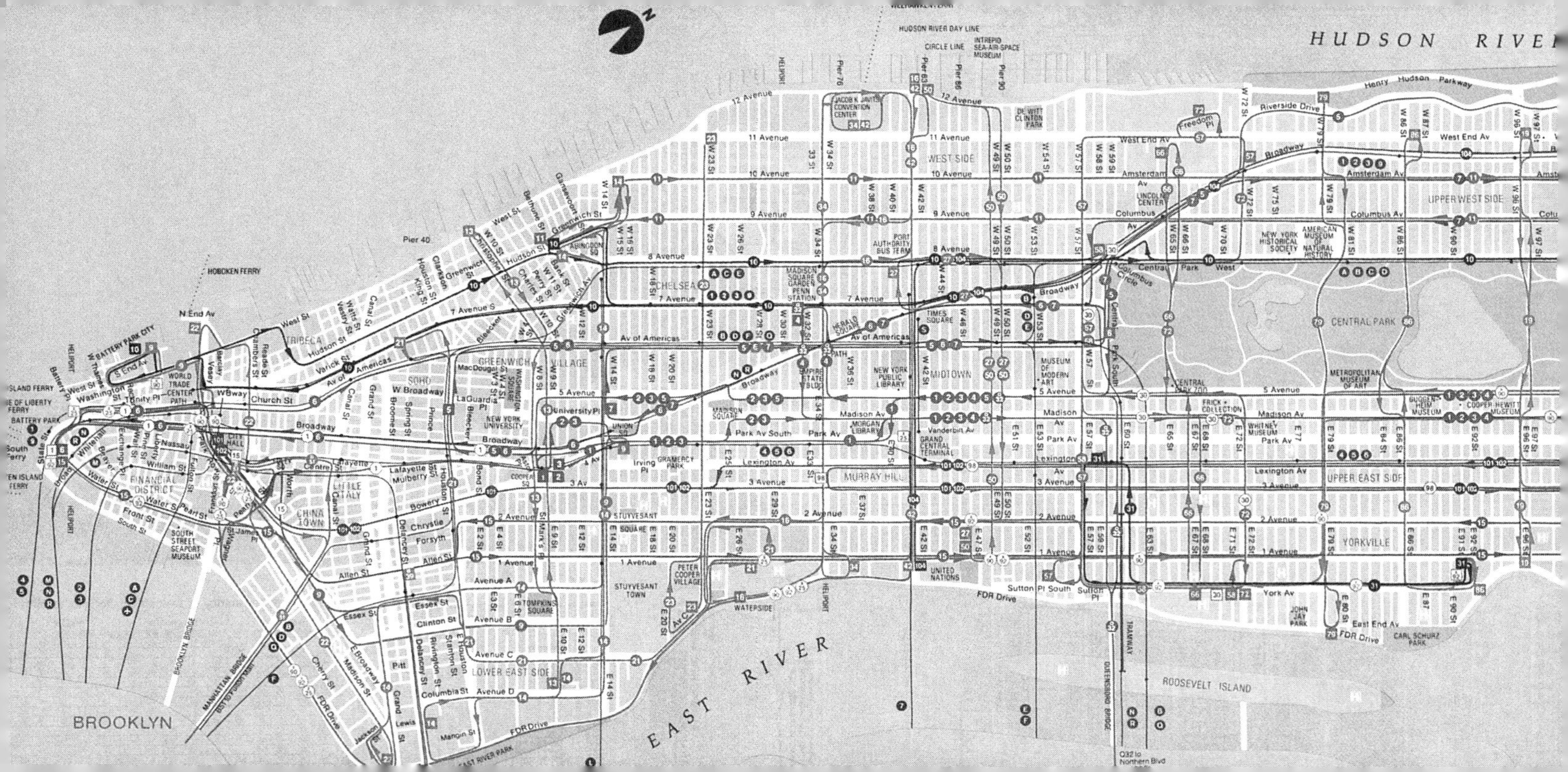

HUDSON RIVER
EAST RIVER
BROOKLYN
CENTRAL PARK
UPPER WEST SIDE
UPPER EAST SIDE
YORKVILLE
ROOSEVELT ISLAND
MIDTOWN
WEST SIDE
CHELSEA
GREENWICH VILLAGE
SOHO
TRIBECA
LITTLE ITALY
CHINA TOWN
LOWER EAST SIDE
FINANCIAL DISTRICT
MURRAY HILL
STUYVESANT TOWN
QUEENSBORO BRIDGE
MANHATTAN BRIDGE
BROOKLYN BRIDGE

32

MAJOR CAR RENTAL AGENCIES

AVIS
(800) 331-1212

1 127 East 83rd St.
2 216 West 76th St.
3 10 East 64th St.
4 156 West 54th St.
5 240 East 54th St.
6 217 East 43rd St.
7 460 West 42nd St.
8 64 East 11th St.
9 One World Trade Center
10 345 South End Ave.
(Gateway Plaza)

BUDGET
(800) 527-0700

11 234 West 85th St.
12 207 West 76th St.
13 403 East 65th St.
14 322 West 57th St.
15 225 East 43rd St.
16 14-16 West 31st St.
17 160 West 10th St.

HERTZ
(800) 654-3131

18 412 East 90th St.
19 210 West 77th St.
20 349 East 76th St.
21 327 East 64th St.
22 128 West 55th St.
23 310 East 48th St.
24 222 East 40th St.
25 250 West 34th Street
26 150 East 24th St.
27 Three World Trade Center
(Vista International Hotel)

NATIONAL
(800) 328-4567

28 305 East 80th St.
29 219 West 77th St.
30 337 East 64th St.
31 148 West 48th St.
32 318 East 48th St.
33 142 East 31st St.
34 21 East 12th St.
35 111 Washington St.

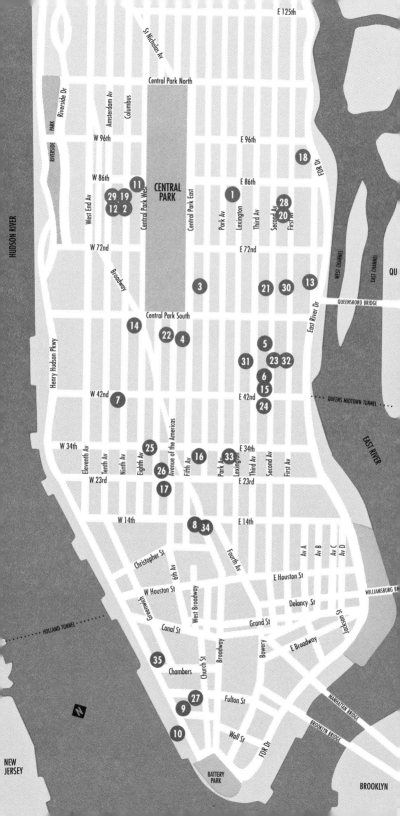

CITY SPORTS' FITNESS CENTERS

You can have your own personal trainer at the Sports Training Institute, or a high profile workout at the trendy Vertical Club. If you only want an hour or so of aerobics and exercise classes, consider places like Body Design by Gilda and The Lotte Berk Method.

1 Aerobics West Fitness Club
131 West 86th St.
787-3356

2 Athletic Complex
3 Park Ave.
686-1085

3 Atrium Club
115 East 57th St.
826-9640

4 Battery Park Swim & Fitness Center
375 South End Ave.
321-1117

5 Body Art
1017 3rd Ave.
593-5771

6 Body Design by Gilda
187 East 79th St.
737-8440

7 65 West 70th St.
799-8540

8 139 East 57th St.
759-7966

9 Cardio Fitness Center
885 Third Ave.
888-2120

10 Chelsea Racquet & Fitness Club
45 West 18th St.
807-8899

11 Club La Raquette
119 West 56th St.
245-1144

12 Competitive Edge
151 West 19th St.
691-1166

13 Downtown Athletic Club
19 West St.
425-7000

14 Excelsior Club
301 East 57th St.
688-5280

15 Executive Fitness Center
3 World Trade Center
466-9266

16 Fifth Ave. Racquet & Fitness Club
404 Fifth Ave.
594-3120

17 Hudson Health Club
353 West 57th St.
586-8630

18 The Lotte Berk Method
23 East 67th St.
288-6613

19 Manhattan Plaza Health Club
450 West 43rd St.
563-7001

20 New York Health & Racquet Club
20 East 50th St.
593-1500
Call for other locations.

21 New York Sports Club
61 West 62nd St.
265-0995

22 Paris Health Club
752 West End Ave.
749-3500

23 Plus One Fitness
106 Crosby St.
334-1116

24 One World Financial Center
945-2525

25 Printing House Racquet Club
421 Hudson St.
243-3777

26 Pumping Iron Gym
320 East 94th St.
996-5444

27 Radu's
41 West 57th St.
759-9617

28 SoHo Training Center
110 Greene St.
219-2018

29 Sports Training Institute
239 East 49th St.
752-7111

30 The Vertical Club
335 Madison Ave.
983-5320

31 330 East 61st St.
355-5100

32 Yorkville Total Fitness
1623 Third Ave.
410-2228

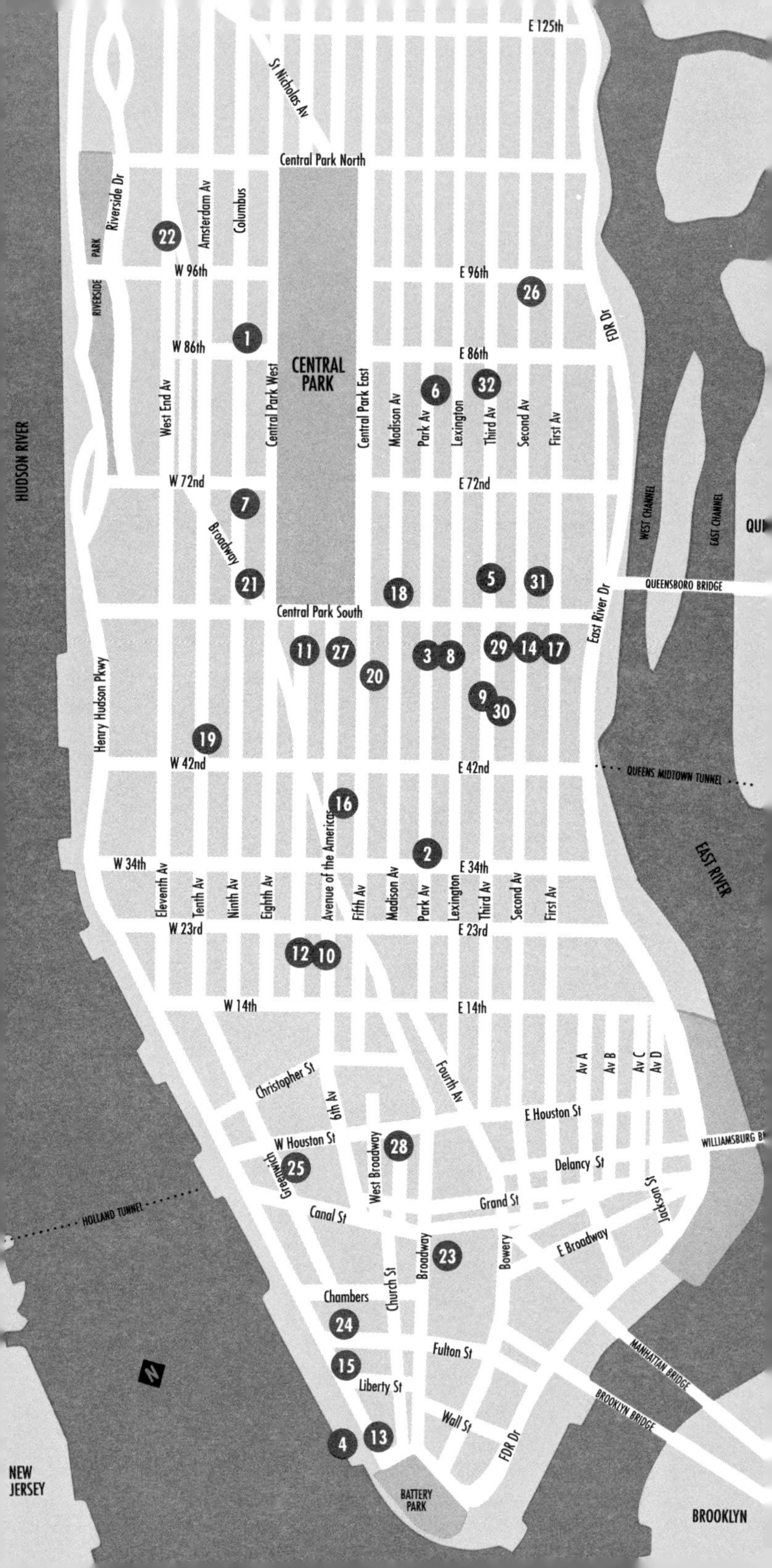

E 125th
St Nicholas Av
Central Park North
Riverside Dr
PARK
Amsterdam Av
Columbus
22
W 96th
E 96th
26
RIVERSIDE
1
W 86th
E 86th
CENTRAL PARK
FDR Dr
6
32
West End Av
Central Park West
Central Park East
Madison Av
Park Av
Lexington
Third Av
Second Av
First Av
HUDSON RIVER
W 72nd
E 72nd
7
Broadway
WEST CHANNEL
EAST CHANNEL
QU
21
18
5
31
QUEENSBORO BRIDGE
Central Park South
East River Dr
11
27
3
8
29
14
17
20
9
30
Henry Hudson Pkwy
19
W 42nd
E 42nd
QUEENS MIDTOWN TUNNEL
16
2
EAST RIVER
W 34th
E 34th
Eleventh Av
Tenth Av
Ninth Av
Eighth Av
Avenue of the Americas
Fifth Av
Madison Av
Park Av
Lexington
Third Av
Second Av
First Av
W 23rd
E 23rd
12
10
W 14th
E 14th
Fourth Av
Av A
Av B
Av C
Av D
Christopher St
6th Av
E Houston St
W Houston St
28
WILLIAMSBURG BR
25
Greenwich
West Broadway
Delancy St
Jackson St
Grand St
HOLLAND TUNNEL
Canal St
23
Broadway
Church St
Bowery
E Broadway
Chambers
24
Fulton St
MANHATTAN BRIDGE
15
Liberty St
BROOKLYN BRIDGE
Wall St
4
13
FDR Dr
N
NEW JERSEY
BATTERY PARK
BROOKLYN

34 NEW YORK CITY MARATHON©

What makes the New York City Marathon what it is, is
Central Park—the home of the Marathon, the base of the
Marathon. With its perfect 6.2-mile loop, and 1.6-mile path
around the reservoir, it's almost as if Olmsted designed the
park specifically for runners.

London has Hyde Park. Moscow has Gorky Park. But
we have Central Park—the granddaddy of them all.

FRED LEBOW, *President*, New York Road Runners Club

For information on the New
York City Marathon and
other runners' events in the
New York area, contact:

New York Road Runners
Club
9 East 89th Street
860-4455
Open M-F, 10am-9pm;
Sat, 10am-5pm; Sun, 10-3pm.
*Recorded information at
other times.*

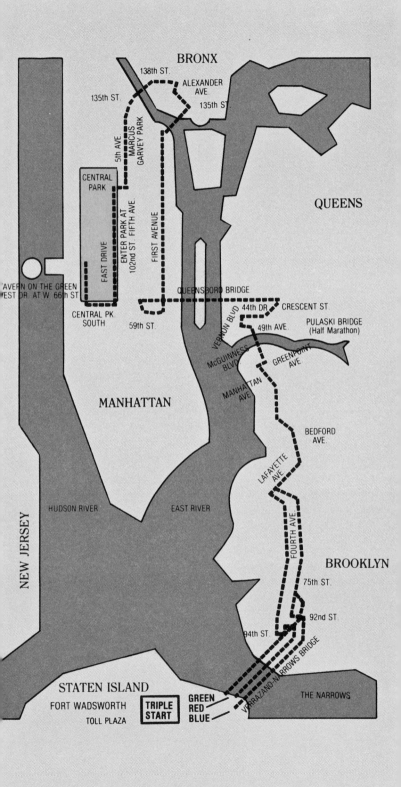

35 CENTRAL PARK

"The dominant and justifying purpose of Central Park was conceived to be that of permanently affording, in the densely populated central portion of an immense metropolis, a means to certain kinds of refreshment of the mind and nerves which most city dwellers greatly need and which they are known to derive in large measure from the enjoyment of suitable scenery."

FREDERICK LAW OLMSTED, SR., *Co-designer with Calvert Vaux of Central Park, originally called Greensward, completed in 1873.*

1 Alice in Wonderland Statue at 75th St.

2 The Arsenal at 64th St.
Art gallery, 360-8111

3 Belvedere Castle at 79th St.

4 Bethesda Fountain at 72nd St.

5 Bow Bridge at 73rd St.

6 Carriage rides at Central Park South
246-0520

7 Children's Zoo at 64th St.
408-0271

8 Conservatory Garden at 105th St.

9 The Dairy at 65th St.*
397-3156

10 Delacorte Theater at 80th St.
New York Shakespeare Festival, 598-7100

11 Friedsam Carousel at 65th St.
879-0244

12 Great Lawn at 84th St.
Ball Fields, 480-0205

13 Heckscher Playground at 62nd St.
Ball Fields, 480-0205
Puppet Theater, 397-3162

14 Kerbs Model Boathouse at 74th St.
360-8133

15 Lasker Pool/Rink at 107th St.
397-3106

16 Loeb Boathouse at 74th St.
Bike rentals, 861-4137
Cafe, 517-2233
Rowboat and gondola rentals, 517-2233

17 North Meadow at 98th St.
Ball Fields, 480-0205

18 The Obelisk (Cleopatra's Needle) at 81st St.

19 Police Precinct House at 86th St.

20 Shakespeare Garden at 79th St.

21 Swiss Cottage at 79th St.
Marionette Theater, 988-9093

22 Tavern-on-the-Green at 67th St.
873-3200

23 Tennis Courts at 95th St.
360-8204

24 The Terrace at 71st St.

25 Wollman Rink at 63rd St.
517-4800

26 The Central Park Zoo at 64th St.
439-6538
(Also see *The Central Park Zoo*, map #3)

The Dairy is the information center for all special programs in the park. You can call them at 397-3156, Tue-Sun, 11am-5pm; F, 1pm-5pm. The Dairy closes at 4pm from October 15-February 15.

NOTE: *The Urban Park Rangers provide guided tours of the park. Call 427-4040*

Cathedral Pkwy
Central Park North
E 110th St

Harlem Meer

W 106th St
E 106th St

15
8

Great Hill

The Pool

North Meadow

WEST DRIVE

EAST DRIVE

East Meadow

17

W 96th St
E 96th St

23

Fifth Ave
Madison Ave
Park Ave
Lexington Ave
Third Ave

The Reservoir

W 86th St
E 86th St

19

12 The Great Lawn

Metropolitan Museum of Art

American Museum of Natural History

18

10

W 79th St
E 79th St

21 **20**

3

The Ramble

Conservatory Water

1

14

16

The Lake

5

Amsterdam Ave
Columbus Ave
Central Park West

W 72nd St
E 72nd St

4

24

Sheep Meadow

WEST DRIVE

The Mall

EAST DRIVE

½ Mile
800 Meters

22

W 66th St

9

7

E 65th St

Lincoln Center

11

26

2

13

Ten minute walk

25

The Pond

6

Columbus Circle
Central Park South
E 59th St
Grand Army Plaza

36

BEST PUBLIC SCULPTURE I
(Above 42nd Street)

Public sculpture just happens and is best when we least expect it. Works catch us by surprise, drawing us into a space or commanding our attention from afar. They can be playful or provocative, subtle or bold, about history or human behavior. They are mediators between the past and present, between the built environment and people.

MICHELE COHEN, Art Historian, *Co-author with Margot Gayle*, Manhattan's Outdoor Sculpture

1   Atlas, 1937
    By Lee Lawrie
    Rockefeller Center
    630 Fifth Ave.
    One of the best examples of its type.

2   Carl Schurz Monument, 1909-13
    By Karl Bitter
    Morningside Dr. and 116th St.
    A total design that artfully combines drama with utility.

3   Ceiling and Waterfall for 666 Fifth Ave., 1955-57
    By Isamu Noguchi
    Passageway of 666 Fifth Ave.
    A combination of falling water and flickering light.

4   Companions, 1985
    By William King
    49th St. at Second Ave.
    Aluminum plate figures locked in greeting.

5   Continuum, 1956
    By José de Rivera
    711 Third Ave. bet. 44th and 45th Sts.
    Inconspicuous but elegant. A play of liquid light against the stainless steel vestibule.

6   Le Guichet, 1963
    By Alexander Calder
    Lincoln Center
    Like a fantastic spider, Le Guichet straddles the plaza.

7   Le Marteleur, 1886
    By Constantin-Emile Meunier
    Columbia University, at the entrance to the engineering building. *A monument to labor.*

8   Lions, 1911
    By Edward Clark Potter
    New York Public Library at 42nd St. and Fifth Ave.
    Beloved landmarks, affectionately known as "Patience" and "Fortitude."

9   Neon for 42nd St, 1979-81
    By Stephen Antonakos
    440 West 42nd St.
    Four incomplete circles of red and blue neon tubes, arcing lyrically in gestural lines.

10 News, 1940
    By Isamu Noguchi
    50 Rockefeller Plaza
    A dynamic tour de force and one of Noguchi's last figurative works.

11 The Sherman Monument, 1892-1903
    By Augustus Saint-Gaudens
    Grand Army Plaza
    Fifth Ave. at 59th St.
    Recently regilded, and among America's most lavish Beaux-Art monuments.

12 Stephen Wise Towers Playground Sculpture, 1964
    By Constantino Nivola
    Playground bet. 90th and 91st Sts., Columbus and Amsterdam Aves.
    These horses await their young riders

13 Still Hunt, 1881-83
    By Edward Kemeys
    Central Park
    East Drive at 76th St.
    Beware all joggers. This panther is ready to spring.

14 Transportation, 1912-14
    By Jules-Felix Coutan
    42nd St. facade of Grand Central Terminal
    A stupendous sculptural clock surmounting the entrance to New York's most elegant gateway.

15 Urban Plaza South, 1985-86
    By Scott Burton
    51st St. at Sixth Ave.
    Sculpture or furniture?

37

BEST PUBLIC SCULPTURE II (42nd Street and Below)

1 Alamo, 1966-1967
By Bernard Rosenthal
Astor Place bet. Lafayette St.
and Fourth Ave.
*One of New York's most
popular public sculptures.*

2 Alfred E. Smith Memorial
Flagpole Base, 1946
By Paul Manship
Governor Smith Memorial
Park at Catherine and
Cherry Sts.
*An atypical flagpole pedestal,
both sophisticated and
whimsical.*

3 Buffalo Hunt, 1914-16
By Charles Cary Rumsey
Entrance arch to Manhattan
Bridge
*An unusual theme for a New
York City Bridge.*

4 Chase Manhattan Bank Plaza
Sunken Garden, 1961-64
By Isamu Noguchi
One Chase Manhattan Plaza
*A palpable imaginary
landscape.*

5 The Commuters, 1980
By George Segal
Port Authority Bus Terminal,
South Wing waiting room.
*A monument to ordinary
urbanites.*

6 The Fables of La Fontaine,
1954
By Mary Callery
P.S. 34, 720 East 12th St. at
Ave. D
*Though little known, a neigh-
borhood bright spot.*

7 Farragut Monument, 1880
By Augustus Saint-Gaudens
Madison Square Park
*Saint-Gaudens' first major
public monument. It changed
the course of American mon-
umental sculpture.*

8 The Four Continents,
1903-07
By Daniel Chester French
United States Custom House,
Bowling Green bet. State and
Whitehall Sts.
*Majestic personifications,
among French's best works.*

9 Group of Four Trees, 1972
By Jean Dubuffet
One Chase Manhattan Plaza
An escape from reality.

10 Horace Greeley, 1890
By John Quincy Adams Ward
City Hall Park
*A probing, psychological
study.*

11 James Gordon Bennett
Memorial, 1939-40
By Antonin Jean Paul Carles
Herald Square
*Make sure you come on the
hour, when "Stuff" and
"Gruff" appear to strike the
bell.*

12 South Cove, 1984-89
Mary Miss, Sculptor
Stanton Eckstut, Architect
Susan Child, Landscape
Architect
Battery Park City at southern
tip of the esplanade.
*A place between land and
water.*

13 Union Square Drinking
Fountain, 1881
By Karl Rudolph Donndorf
Union Square West
*A rare civic amenity of
Victorian vintage.*

14 Untitled, 1973
By Forrest Myers
North wall of 599 Broadway
*Subtle and unexpected, a bal-
ance between surface and
structure.*

38

RESTAURANTS WITH A VIEW I (Looking Out)

If dining above the clouds appeals to you, Windows on the World is the place to go. Perched 107 floors atop the World Trade Center, Windows on the World overlooks Manhattan, its suburbs, and New Jersey. Next door—for those who prefer drinking to dining at high altitudes—the City Lights Bar & Hors d'Oeuvrerie hails Miss Liberty and the New York Harbor.

Below are some other great views of the city:

1 The Boathouse Cafe
Loeb Boathouse, Central
Park Lake at 74th St.
Enter at 72nd Street; trolley
service available.
517-2233

2 City Lights Bar & Hors
d'Oeuvrerie at Windows on
the World
One World Trade Center
107th Floor
938-1111

3 Hudson River Club
4 World Financial Center
Mezzanine Level
786-1500

4 Nirvana
30 Central Park South
15th Floor
486-5700

5 Rainbow Promenade and
Rainbow Room
RCA Building
30 Rockefeller Plaza
65th Floor
632-5000

6 River Café
One Water St.
Across the East River, next
to the Brooklyn Bridge
(718) 522-5200

7 Tavern-on-the-Green
Central Park West at West
67th St.
873-3200

8 The Terrace
Butler Hall
400 West 119th St.
Top Floor
666-9490

9 Top of the Sixes
666 Fifth Ave.
39th Floor
757-6662

10 Top of the Tower
Beekman Tower
3 Mitchell Pl., First Ave.
and 49th St.
26th Floor
355-7300

11 The View Restaurant
Marriott Marquis Hotel
1535 Broadway
47th Floor
704-8900

12 The Water Club
East River at East 30th St.
683-3333

13 Water's Edge Restaurant
East River Yacht Club
East River and 44th Dr.
Long Island City, Queens
(718) 482-0033

14 World Yacht
Pier 62
Hudson River at West
23rd St.
929-7090

E 125th

8

S Nicholas Av

Central Park North

Riverside Dr

RIVERSIDE PARK

Amsterdam Av

Columbus

W 96th

E 96th

W 86th

E 86th

CENTRAL PARK

West End Av

Central Park West

Central Park East

Madison Av

Park Av

Lexington

Third Av

Second Av

First Av

FDR Dr

1

W 72nd

E 72nd

Broadway

7

WEST CHANNEL

EAST CHANNEL

QUEEN

Central Park South

4

East River Dr

QUEENSBORO BRIDGE

9

11

5

10

13

HUDSON RIVER

Henry Hudson Pkwy

W 42nd

E 42nd

QUEENS MIDTOWN TUNNEL

W 34th

Eleventh Av

Tenth Av

Ninth Av

Eighth Av

Seventh Av

Avenue of the Americas

Fifth Av

Madison Av

Park Av

Lexington

Third Av

Second Av

First Av

E 34th

EAST RIVER

W 23rd

E 23rd

14

12

W 14th

E 14th

Christopher St

6th Av

Fourth Av

Av A

Av B

Av C

Av D

Greenwich

W Houston St

West Broadway

E Houston St

HOLLAND TUNNEL

Delancy St

WILLIAMSBURG BRIDGE

Canal St

Grand St

Jackson St

Broadway

Bowery

E Broadway

Chambers

Church St

MANHATTAN BRIDGE

3

2

Fulton St

Liberty St

BROOKLYN BRIDGE

Wall St

FDR Dr

6

BATTERY PARK

BROOKLYN

W
RSEY

39

RESTAURANTS WITH A VIEW II (Looking Around)

People watching—New York's favorite pastime. Here are the best spots in the city (where the food's great, too).

1 150 Wooster
150 Wooster St.
995-1010

2 Alison on Dominick Street
38 Dominick St. bet. Varick
and Hudson Sts.
727-1188

3 Arcadia
21 East 62nd St.
223-2900

4 Bice
7 East 54th Street
688-1999

5 Cafe Luxembourg
200 West 70th St.
873-7411

6 Columbus
201 Columbus Ave.
799-8090

7 Delia's
197 East 3rd St.
254-9184

8 Elaine's
1703 Second AvEast
534-8114

9 Elio's
1621 Second Ave.
772-2242

10 Florent
69 Gansevoort St.
989-5779

11 The Four Seasons
99 East 52nd St.
754-9494

12 Gotham Bar & Grill
12 East 12th St.
620-4020

13 Indochine
430 Lafayette St.
505-5111

14 Jerry's
101 Prince St.
966-9464

15 Jim McMullen's
1341 Third Ave.
861-4700

16 La Grenouille
3 East 52 St.
752-1495

17 Le Cirque
58 East 65th St.
794-9292

18 Le Madri
168 West 18th St.
727-8022

19 Le Relais
712 Madison Ave.
751-5108

20 Lucky Strike
59 Grand St.
941-0479

21 Michael's
24 West 55th St.
767-0555

22 Mortimer's
1057 Lexington Ave.
517-6400

23 Mr. Chow
324 East 57th St.
751-9030

24 Punsch
11 West 60th St.
767-0606

25 Remi
1325 Sixth Ave.
581-4242

26 Russian Tea Room
150 West 57th St.
265-0947

27 Sardi's
234 West 44th St.
221-8440

28 Sette Mezzo
969 Lexington Ave.
472-0400

29 Trattoria dell'Arte
900 Seventh Ave.
245-9800

30 TriBeCa Grill
375 Greenwich St.
941-3900

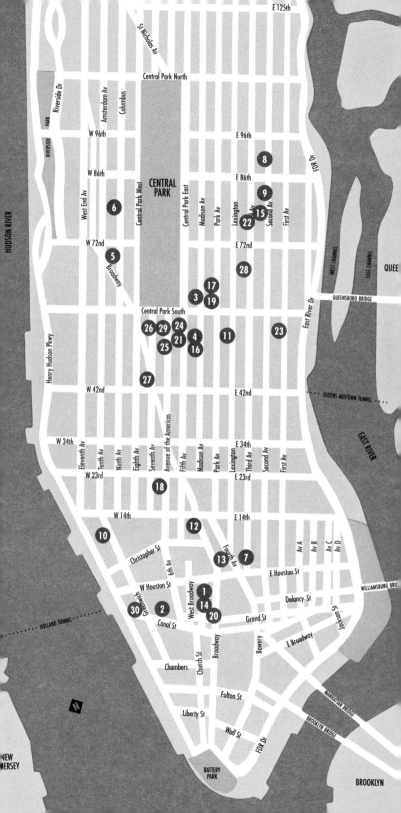

40

EEYORE'S I
(Children's Excursions)

Having a kid or two in tow who require amusement is one of the best ways for grownups to be drawn away from their to-work-and-back syndrome and appreciate this gigantic real-life theme park we live in.

Present-day New York reminds me of Dickens' description of London seen through a young boy's eyes 'an enchanting cacophony of human activity.'

JOEL FRAM, *Owner, Eeyore's Books for Children*

1 Climb to the top of Riverside Church among the clarion bells.
490 Riverside Dr. at 122nd St.
222-5900

2 The Little Red Lighthouse, just south of the George Washington Bridge in Manhattan, on which the classic children's story, *The Little Red Lighthouse and the Great Grey Bridge* is based.

3 New York Public Library Donnell Library Center Central Children's Room
20 West 53rd St.
621-0636

4 Observation Deck Two World Trade Center Church and Liberty Streets.

5 Riverside Park/79th St. Boat Basin
Riverside Dr. at 79th St.

6 Roosevelt Island
Take tramway at First Ave. & 59th St.; walk through the town and north to the lighthouse at the northern tip of the island.

7 Staten Island Ferry/Battery Park
Foot of Whitehall St. at Battery Park
(718) 727-2508

8 Statue of Liberty Liberty Island
363-3200
Take ferry at Battery Park.

9 United Nations
405 East 42nd St.
963-7713

ICE SKATING

10 Lasker Ice Skating Rink Central Park at 107th St.
397-3106

11 Skating Rink Rockefeller Center
757-5730

12 Sky Rink
450 West 33rd St.
695-6555

13 Wollman Ice Skating Rink Central Park at 63rd St.
517-4800

MUSEUMS

14 American Museum of Natural History
Central Park West at 79th St.
769-5000

15 AT & T Infoquest Center
550 Madison Ave.
605-5140

16 Children's Museum of Manhattan
212 West 83rd St.
721-1234

17 Hayden Planetarium Central Park West at 81st St.
769-5900

18 Intrepid Sea Air & Space Museum
Pier 86
Twelfth Ave. at 46th St.
245-2533

19 Museum of Holography
11 Mercer St.
925-0581

20 Museum of the American Indian
3753 Broadway at 155th St.
283-2420

21 Museum of the City of New York
Fifth Ave. bet. 103rd and 104th Sts.
534-1672

22 New York Fire Museum
278 Spring St. bet. Varick and Hudson Sts.
691-1303

41

EEYORE'S II
(Toy, Hobby, and Doll Shops)

1   America's Hobby Center
146 West 22nd St.
675-8922

2   Big City Kites
1201 Lexington Ave.
472-7148

3   Children of Paradise
154 Bleecker St.
473-7148

4   Doll House Antics
1308 Madison Ave.
876-2288

5   Dolls and Dreams
1421 Lexington Ave.
876-2434

6   Enchanted Forest
85 Mercer St.
925-6677

7   FAO Schwarz
767 Fifth Ave.
644-9400

8   Forbidden Planet
227 East 59th St.
751-4386

9   821 Broadway
473-1576

10   Jan's Hobby Shop
1431A York Ave.
861-5075

11   Kiddie City
Union Square East
629-3070

12   Last Woundup
869 Broadway
529-4197

13   290 Columbus Ave.
787-3388

14   Manhattan Doll House
176 Ninth Ave.
989-5220

15   Mary Arnold Toys
962 Lexington Ave.
744-8510

16   Penny Whistle
1283 Madison Ave.
369-3868

17   448 Columbus Ave.
873-9090

18   132 Spring St.
925-2088

19   Polk's Model Craft Hobby
Shop
314 Fifth Ave.
279-9034

20   The Red Caboose
16 West 45th St.
575-0155

21   Star Magic
275 Amsterdam Ave.
769-2020

22   743 Broadway
228-7770

23   Toy Park
112 East 86th St.
427-6611

24   626 Columbus Ave.
769-3880

25   The Train Shop
23 West 45th St.
730-0409

26   West Side Kids
498 Amsterdam Ave.
496-7282

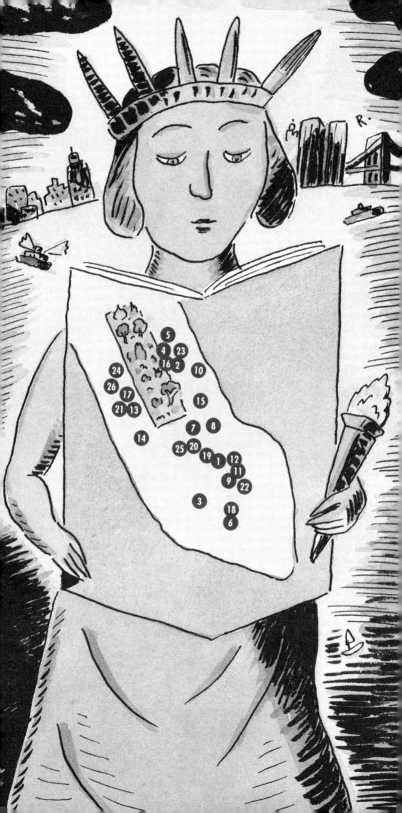

42

EEYORE'S III
(Children's Restaurants, Bookstores, and Clothing Stores)

RESTAURANTS

1 Hamburger Harry's
145 West 45th St.
840-2756

2 157 Chambers St.
267-4446

3 Old Fashioned Mr. Jennings
Ice Cream Parlor
12 West 55th St.
582-2238

4 Rumpelmeyer's at the
St. Moritz
50 Central Park South
755-5800

5 Serendipity
225 East 60th St.
838-3531

6 Swensen's Ice Cream of
Mercer Square
14 West 4th St.
674-7664

7 1246 Second Ave.
879-8686

CHILDREN'S BOOKS

8 Books of Wonder
132 Seventh Ave.
989-3270

9 464 Hudson St.
645-8006

10 Eeyore's Books for Children
25 East 83rd St.
988-3404

11 2212 Broadway
362-0634

12 Forbidden Planet
227 East 59th St.
751-4386

13 821 Broadway
473-1576

14 Storyland
1369 Third Ave.
517-6951

15 West Side Comics
107 West 86th St.
724-0432

MUSEUM SHOPS WITH GOOD CHILDREN'S BOOKS

16 The Cathedral of St. John the
Divine
Amsterdam Ave. at 112th St.
222-7200

17 The Children's Museum
of Manhattan
212 West 83rd St.
721-1234

18 The Pierpont Morgan
Library
29 East 36th St.
685-0610

19 The New York Historical
Society
170 Central Park West
873-3400

20 The New York Public
Library
Main Branch
Fifth Ave. at 42 St.
930-0641

CHILDREN'S CLOTHING
(Also see *Along Orchard Street*, map #48, for discount children's clothing.)

21 Bebe Thompson
98 Thompson St.
925-1122

22 Cerutti
807 Madison Ave. bet. 67th
and 68th Sts.
737-7540

23 Citykids
130 Seventh Ave. bet. 17th
and 18th Sts.
620-0120

24 Greenstone and Cie.
442 Columbus Ave. bet. 81st
and 82nd Sts.
580-4322

25 1184 Madison Ave.
427-1665

43

HOLLYWOOD ON THE HUDSON

I can never cross 34th Street and Fifth Avenue without remembering what happened to Irene Dunne in the 1939 movie, *Love Affair*. She and Charles Boyer have had a shipboard romance, but they decide to test their love by separating for a year, after which they plan to meet at the top of the Empire State Building. If either decides not to come, the affair is over.

Boyer arrives first, but when Dunne gets to the corner of 34th and Fifth, she steps into the street while longingly looking up at the building. She's hit by a bus, and it takes them several reels to reunite.

DONALD ALBRECHT, *Curator of Exhibitions*, American Museum of the Moving Image

1   55 Central Park West
    *Building used for many exte-
    riors of Sigourney Weaver's
    home in Ghostbusters. The
    temple on top of the building
    was achieved by combining a
    matte painting for long shots,
    a miniature for medium shots,
    and a full-scale construction
    for close-ups.*

2   The American Museum of the
    Moving Image
    36-01 35th Ave.
    Astoria, Queens
    (718) 784-0077
    *The first American museum
    devoted to film, television,
    and video.*

3   Brill Building
    1141 Broadway
    *Penthouse of Burt Lancaster,
    as J.J. Hunsacker, in* Sweet
    Smell of Success.

4   Central Park
    *Ryan O'Neal and Ali McGraw
    walk across the Great Lawn in*
    Love Story, *Sandy Dennis and
    Jack Lemmon get mugged in*
    The Out-of-Towners, *and
    Dustin Hoffman runs around
    the reservoir in* Marathon Man.

5   The Dakota
    1 West 72nd St.
    Mia Farrow's apartment in
    Rosemary's Baby.

6   The Empire State Building
    34th St. at Fifth Ave.
    *Irene Dunne gets hit by a bus
    and is crippled while crossing
    the street to meet Charles
    Boyer in the 1939 film* Love
    Affair.

7   Fifth Ave. at about 63rd St.
    In the 1937 film Easy Living,
    *a sable coat falls from a swank
    penthouse onto an underpaid
    secretary (Jean Arthur) riding
    a bus. Her life is transformed
    when everyone assumes that
    she is as wealthy as she looks.*

8   Frank E. Campbell Funeral
    Home
    1076 Madison Ave.
    288-3500
    *Site of the final services for
    many movie celebrities,
    including Judy Garland, Joan
    Crawford, Montgomery Clift,
    and James Cagney. Campbell's
    original parlor, at Broadway
    and 66th St., hosted Rudolph
    Valentino's funeral in 1926.*

9   Grand Central Station
    *Robert Walker meets Judy
    Garland at the right-hand
    stairwell on the Main
    Concourse in Vincent
    Minnelli's* The Clock.

10 Kaufman-Astoria Studios
    34-12 36th St.
    Astoria, Queens
    (718) 392-5600
    *Across from the American
    Museum of the Moving
    Image (above). Paramount
    Picture's East Coast facility in
    the 1920s and today the home
    of* The Cosby Show.

11 Library for the Performing Arts
    Lincoln Center
    870-1630
    *The single best source for film
    and television research.*

12 The Museum of Modern Art
11 West 53rd St.
708-9400
Has one of the world's great film collections and two excellent screening facilities.

13 The Rainbow Room
RCA Building
30 Rockefeller Center
632-5100
With its double curving stairway straight out of Astaire and Rogers' "Never Gonna Dance" number from 1936's Swing Time, *the Rainbow Room makes visitors feel like movie stars.*

14 The Russian Tea Room
150 West 57th St.
265-0947
A favorite lunch spot for movie and television dealmakers, and the restaurant in Tootsie *where Dustin Hoffman-in-drag meets his agent, played by Sydney Pollack, the film's director.*

15 The Seagram Building
375 Park Ave.
The post-war, steel-and-glass tower used to express corporate power and prestige, from Joan Crawford's publishing firm in The Best of Everything *to the office of Marlo Thomas's boyfriend in* That Girl.

16 Sutton Place at 57th St.
One of the most romantic of New York locations. Judy Holliday sings "The Party's Over" on MGM's recreation of the site in Bells Are Ringing, *while just to the north Woody Allen and Diane Keaton watch the sun come up in* Manhattan.

17 Tiffany & Co.
727 Fifth Ave.
755-8000
Audrey Hepburn's favorite store in Breakfast at Tiffany's.

18 The Ziegfeld Theater
141 West 54th St.
765-7600
The city's best movie theater.

AVANT GARDE FILMS

19 Anthology Film Archives
32 Second Ave.
505-5181

20 The Collective for Living Cinema
41 White St.
925-2111

21 Millennium Film Workshop
66 East 4th St.
673-0090

22 The Public Theater
425 Lafayette St.
598-7171

MIDNIGHT MOVIES

23 Angelika Film Center
18 West Houston St.
995-2000

24 Bleecker Street Cinemas
144 Bleecker St.
674-2560

25 Eighth Street Playhouse
52 West 8th St.
674-6515

26 Waverly Twin
323 Sixth Ave.
929-8037

POSTERS AND MEMORABILIA

27 Motion Picture Arts Gallery
133 East 58th St.
10th Floor
223-1009
Original posters and lobby cards from motion pictures for sale.

28 Movie Star News
134 West 18th St.
620-8160
Boasts the world's largest collection of movie posters.

REVIVAL HOUSES

29 Cinema Village
22 East 12th St.
924-3363

30 Film Forum
209 West Houston St.
727-8110

31 Thalia Soho
15 Vandam St.
675-0498

32 Theatre 80 St. Mark's
80 St. Mark's Pl.
254-7400

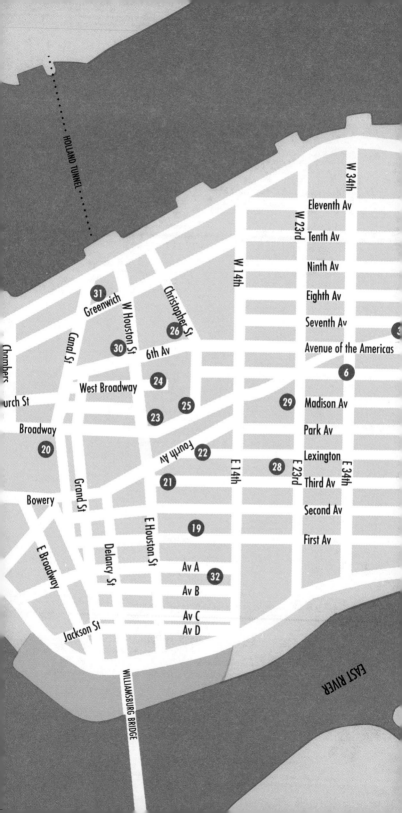

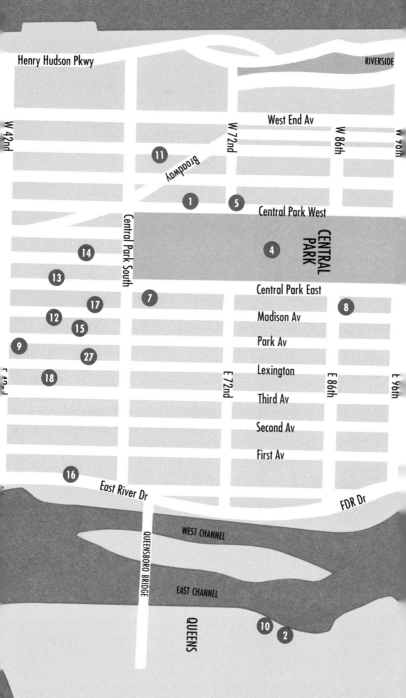

44

THE LIKELIEST PLACES TO GET KILLED

According to New York City Police Department statistics, more than fifty percent of all homicides are committed by someone the victim knows—most frequently, a neighbor.

	PRECINCT	AVERAGE NUMBER OF MURDERS PER YEAR
1	First Precinct	5
2	Fifth Precinct	5
3	Sixth Precinct	6
4	Seventh Precinct	5
5	Ninth Precinct	15
6	Tenth Precinct	7
7	Thirteenth Precinct	5
8	Seventeenth Precinct	2
9	Manhattan South Precinct	14
10	Nineteenth Precinct	7
11	Manhattan North Precinct	16
12	Twentieth Precinct	6
13	Central Park Precinct	2
14	Twenty-third Precinct	25
15	Twenty-fourth Precinct	16
16	Twenty-fifth Precinct	21
17	Twenty-sixth Precinct	7
18	Twenty-eighth Precinct	23
19	Thirtieth Precinct	31
20	Thirty-second Precinct	46
21	Thirty-fourth Precinct	55

New York City Police Department, Crime Analysis Unit, Statistical Reports averaged for years available (1984, 1986, 1987, 1989).

45 MARTHA STEWART'S FOOD STOPS

My route is long, but I am happy to go long distances if that means I am assured of the best farmer's cheese, or the tastiest kielbasa. My 'pit stops' include inexpensive restaurants where I stop for snacks or pick-me-ups after long days of meetings and negotiations.

MARTHA STEWART, *Author and Lifestyle Consultant to* K-Mart Corp.

PROVISIONS

1 Balducci's
424 Sixth Ave.
673-2600
Fresh produce, meat, fish, cheese, bread.

2 Bazzini Nuts
339 Greenwich St.
227-6241
Nuts, dried fruit.

3 Ben's Cheese Shop
181 East Houston St.
254-8290
Best farmer's cheese.

4 Dean & DeLuca
560 Broadway
431-1691
Cheese, produce, kitchen oddities.

5 E.A.T. Gourmet Foods & Cafe
1064 Madison Ave.
772-0022
Cappuccino, sourdough baguettes, seven-grain bread.

6 First Avenue Pierogi & Deli
130 First Ave.
420-9690

7 Grace's Market Place
1237 Third Ave.
737-0600
Bread, produce.

8 Green Village Market
1457 Third Ave.
734-7687
Hard-to-find food items.

9 Kurowycky Meat Products
124 First Ave.
477-0344
The very best Polish kielbasa, Polish ham, kishka.

10 Lobel's Prime Meats
1096 Madison Ave.
737-1372
Aged wild meat, turkey.

11 Murray's Sturgeon Shop
2429 Broadway
724-2650
Terrific smoked fish.

12 Paprikas Weiss
1546 Second Ave.
288-6117
Ground poppy seeds, freshest paprika anywhere.

13 Russ & Daughters
179 East Houston St.
475-4880
Dried fruit, nuts, herring.

14 Salumeria Biellese
376 Eighth Ave.
736-7376
Sausage, homemade pasta, specialities (boudin, andouille).

15 Yonah Schimmel
137 East Houston St.
477-2858
Very best knishes.

RESTAURANTS

16 Joy Luck
57 Mott St.
267-3056
Sunny Fish, crabs with black beans, other authentic dishes.

17 Katz's Delicatessen
205 East Houston St.
254-2246
Wonderful pastrami, brisket, corned beef, turkey sandwiches.

18 Little Cuban Restaurants
bet. 101st and 109th on Broadway
Cuban coffee, rice and beans, Cuban sandwiches.

19 Papaya King
Third Avenue at 86th Street
369-0648
Hot dogs with saurekraut and a papaya-coconut drink.

20 Sylvia's
328 Lenox Ave.
996-0660
Short ribs, sweet potato pie.

JAZZ CLUBS

Jazz is the chamber music of the late 20th century. Its intimacy, and the relationship it forges between performers and audience, is reminiscent of another time—when 'cultured' folk gathered in congenial settings for social and artistic enrichment. While jazz continues to evolve in form and venue, it is, undoubtably, America's most powerful contribution to the music world.

It is important that jazz be heard in settings that insure contact between audience and musician, where background noise level is controlled, and acoustics are reasonably good.

DAVID C. LEVY, *Chancellor,* The New School for Social Research; *Founder,* New School/Jazz and Contemporary Music Program.

TRADITIONAL JAZZ CLUBS

1 Blue Note
131 West 3rd St.
475-8592

2 Fat Tuesdays
190 Third Ave. at 17th St.
533-7902

3 Mich'ael's Pub
211 East 55th St.
758-2272
Woody Allen plays his clarinet here Monday nights.

4 Sweet Basil
88 Seventh Ave. South
242-1785

5 Village Gate
160 Bleecker St. at La Guardia Pl.
475-5120

6 Village Vanguard
178 Seventh Ave.
255-4037
New York's oldest jazz establishment.

BARS/CLUBS FEATURING LIVE MUSIC

7 55 Bar
55 Christopher St.
929-9883

8 Angry Squire
216 Seventh Ave.
242-9066

9 Birdland
2745 Broadway
749-2228

10 Bradley's
70 University Place
473-9700
A tiny bar/restaurant showcasing an astounding array of the world's best jazz musicians.

11 Café Comedy
308 West 58th St.
757-8383
Jazz only on Wednesdays.

12 Carlos No. 1
432 Sixth Ave.
982-3260

13 J's
2581 Broadway bet. 97th and 98th Sts.
2nd Floor
666-3600

14 Knitting Factory
47 East Houston St.
219-3055

15 Red Blazer Too
349 West 46th St.
262-3112

16 SOB's (Sounds of Brazil)
204 Varick St.
243-4940

17 Visiónes
125 MacDougal St.
627-9040

18 West End Gate
2911 Broadway at 114th St.
662-8830

19 Zanzibar and Grill
550 Third Ave.
779-0606

20 Zinno
126 West 13th St.
924-5182

NOTE: Performances and show times vary; call ahead for details.

47 GEOFFREY HOLDER'S HARLEM

Harlem is composed of people from all over the world: Africa, North America, South America, and the Caribbean. These people have magic in their culture: the majesty of the blues, the power of the salsa rhythms. They are splendidly creative.

GEOFFREY HOLDER, *Choreographer, Painter, Actor, Photographer*

1 The Apollo Theater
253 West 125th St.
749-5838

2 Aunt Len's Doll and Toy Museum
6 Hamilton Terrace bet. St. Nicholas and Convent Aves.
926-4172

3 The Black Fashion Museum
155-157 West 126th St.
666-1320

4 Dance Theatre of Harlem
466 West 152nd St. (School)
690-2800
For performance information call 967-3470.

5 The Harlem School of the Arts
645 St. Nicholas Ave. at 141st St.
926-4100

6 Harlem Spirituals
1457 Broadway
302-2594
Spirituals and gospel on Sunday. Soul food and jazz hour on weekends.

7 Harlem Street Gallery International Ltd.
Lenox Ave. at 125th St. at the fence
866-0283
Large outdoor exhibition of Black art.

8 Morris-Jumel Mansion
West 160th St. at Edgecombe Ave.
923-8008
Washington's headquarters during the Battle of Harlem Heights in 1776; later home of French merchant Stephen Jumel and family. Rumored to be haunted. Herb garden.

9 Mr. T's
52 West 125th St.
289-8006
Hair weaving, corn rows, and braiding.

10 National Black Theater
2033 Fifth Ave. at 125th St.
426-5615

11 Powell Gallery
163 West 125th St.
864-4500
Features work of Black and Hispanic artists.

12 Schomburg Center for Research in Black Culture
135th St. at Lenox Ave.
862-4000
Most extensive collection of books, recordings, manuscripts, photographs, and artwork documenting Black culture in United States.

13 "Strivers' Row"
West 138th and 139th Sts. bet. Adam Clayton Powell and Frederick Douglass Blvds.
Builder David King commissioned leading architects to build the King Model Houses, a grouping of row houses and apartments. Intended for white residents, they became homes of successful Blacks in 20s and 30s and became known as "Strivers' Row."

14 Studio Museum in Harlem
144 West 125th St.
864-4500
Permanent collection includes works by post-World War II Black American artists, as well as African and Caribbean works.

BEST RESTAURANTS

15 Hot Pot
2260 Seventh Ave. near 133rd St.
491-5270
Jamaican.

16 Sylvia's
328 Lenox Ave.
996-0660
Delicious barbecue and soul food.

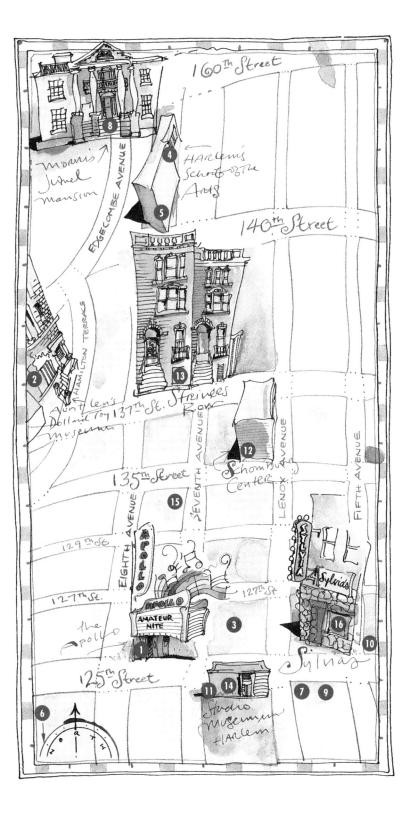

48

ALONG ORCHARD STREET

Once the commerce center of New York's Jewish ghetto, Orchard Street is still the place to hustle for bargains. Now barely changed from the days when merchants aggressively peddled their wares from pushcarts on the crowded street, Orchard north of Canal is lined with small retail shops and outdoor stalls selling affordably-priced designer clothing, household items, and ethnic food.

Take note: many businesses close for the Sabbath on Saturday—some close early Friday—but on Sunday, the area is teeming with activity and the sights and smells of old New York.

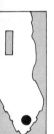

ACCESSORIES

1 Bernard Krieger & Son
316 Grand St.
223-1929
Handkerchiefs and scarves.

2 Fine & Klein
119 Orchard St.
674-6720
Handbags and other leather goods.

CHILDREN'S CLOTHING

3 A&G Children's Wear
261 Broome St.
966-3775
Carter, Bull Frog, Tickle Me, among others.

4 Klein's of Monticello
105 Orchard St.
966-1453
Clothes for the young hipster, including Naf Naf, Bourget, and Trotinette.

5 Little Rascals
101 Orchard St.
226-1680
Traditional clothes from Italy and France.

6 M. Kreinen Sales
301 Grand St.
925-0239
Wide selection of upscale children's clothes.

7 Rice & Breskin
323 Grand St.
925-5515
Well-known infants' and children's clothing.

HOSIERY & LINGERIE

8 AW Kaufman
73 Orchard St.
226-1629
Wide selection, including trousseau department.

9 Goldman & Cohen
54 Orchard St.
966-0737
Bali, Warner, Maidenform available.

10 Lismore Hosiery Co.
334 Grand St.
674-3440
Special house brand, with cotton and silk blends a specialty.

11 Mendel Weiss, Inc.
91 Orchard St.
925-6815
Big selection of well-known lingerie.

12 RC Sultan Ltd.
55 Orchard St.
925-9650,-51
Specializes in Hanes panty hose; men's and women's underwear.

LINENS

13 Ezra Cohen
307 Grand St.
925-7800
Two floors of name brand items for bed and bath.

14 Harris Levy
278 Grand St.
226-3102
Selection of imported linens.

MEN'S CLOTHING

15 Antony
106 Orchard St.
477-0592
First-rate clothes at substantial discounts; designer wear.

16 Bridge Merchandise Corporation
74 Orchard St.
674-6320
Leather goods.

17 Leslie's Bootery
319 Grand St.
431-9196
Bally, Rockport, Cole-Haan among others.

18 Victory Shirt Company
96 Orchard St.
677-2020
Factory direct prices 25% off department stores.

WOMEN'S CLOTHING

19 Berent & Smith
94 Rivington St.
254-0900
Better sportswear and dresses.

20 Breakaway
88 Rivington St.
598-4455

21 125 Orchard St.
475-6660
Ellen Tracy, Harvé Bernard and European designers.

22 Chez Aby
77-79 Delancey St.
431-6135
French and Italian imports.

23 The Dress
103 Stanton St.
473-0237
Minimalist designs by owners Amy Downs and Mary Adams.

24 Fishkin
314 Grand St.

25 318 Grand St.

26 63 Orchard St.
226-6538 (all stores)
Calvin Klein, Liz Claiborne, Adrienne Vittadini available; boot and shoes also.

27 Friedlich, Inc.
196 Orchard St.
254-8899
French and Italian sportswear.

28 Lace Up Shoe Shop
110 Orchard St.
475-8040
Well-known shoe designs (owner refuses to name them) at good discounts.

29 L'Ambiance
86-88 Stanton St.
533-4820
Couture boutique featuring designs by owners Luis Reyna and Michael Martin.

30 Opium
104 Orchard St.
533-8394
Specializes in designer winter coats; European silk imports also.

Map streets: Stanton St, Eldridge St, Allen St, Orchard St, Ludlow St, Rivington St, Delancey St, Broome St, Grand St, Hester St, Canal St

49

FLEA MARKETS AND ANTIQUE BAZAARS

You can find anything from valuable antiques to used car parts at New York's flea markets and antique bazaars. For many New Yorkers, flea marketing has become a weekend ritual.

1   Annex Antiques Fair & Flea Market
    Sixth Avenue bet. 24th and 26th Sts.
    243-5343
    Sat-Sun, 9am-5pm

2   Battery Park Crafts Exhibit
    State St. bet. Bowling Green subway and Pearl St.
    752-8475
    Thur, 11am-6pm (Seasonal)

3   Bryant Park Crafts Show
    42nd St. bet. Fifth and Sixth Aves.
    752-8475
    F, 11am-6pm

4   Irreplaceable Artifacts
    Corner Houston St. and Bowery (under large tent)
    777-2900
    M-F, 10am-6pm;
    Sat-Sun, 11am-5pm
    Auctions, Thur evenings, spring and summer
    Flea market outlet of main store at 14 Second Ave.

5   IS 44 Flea Market
    Columbus Ave. bet. 76th and 77th Sts.
    678-2817
    Sun, 10am-6pm

6   Manhattan Art & Antique Center
    1050 Second Ave.
    355-4400
    Sun, noon-6pm;
    M-Sat, 10:30am-6:15pm

7   Place des Antiquaires
    125 East 57th St.
    758-2709
    Sun, noon-5pm;
    Tue-Sat, 11am-7pm

8   PS 41 Schoolyard
    Greenwich Ave. bet. Sixth and Seventh Ave.
    751-4932
    Sat, 11am-7pm

9   PS 183 Flea Market
    419 East 66th St.
    737-8888
    Sat, 6am-6pm

10 Soho Emporium
    375 West Broadway
    966-7895
    Daily, noon-8pm

11 Tower Market
    Broadway between West 4th and Great Jones Sts.
    (718) 693-8702
    Sat-Sun, 10am-7pm

12 Walter's World Famous Union Square Shoppes
    873 Broadway at 18th St.
    255-0175
    Tue-Sat, 10am-6pm

13 Yorkville Flea Market
    351 East 74th St.
    535-5235
    Sat, 9am-4pm (No market June-August)

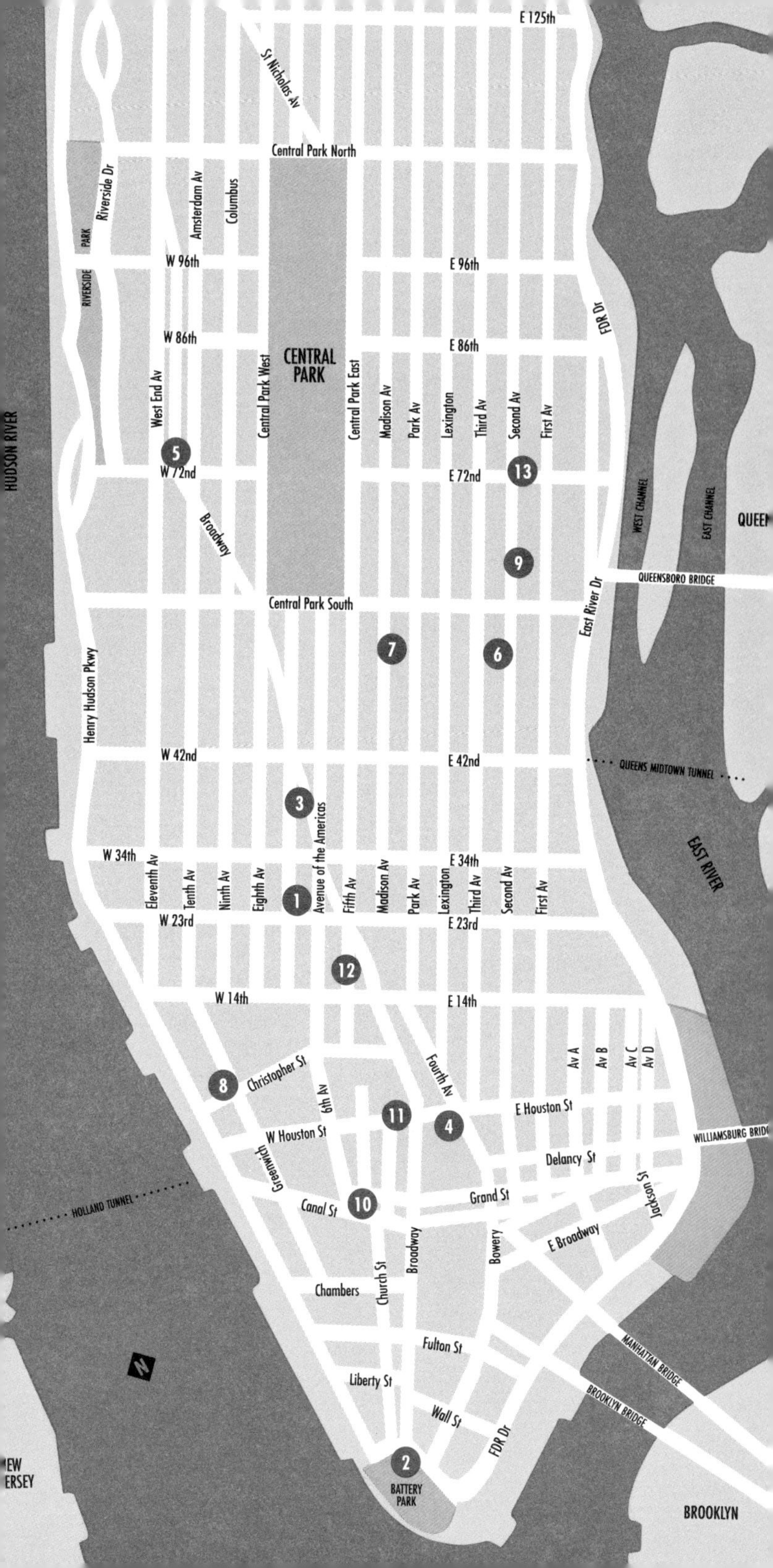
E 125th
St Nicholas Av
Central Park North
Riverside Dr
Amsterdam Av
Columbus
RIVERSIDE
PARK
W 96th
E 96th
FDR Dr
W 86th
E 86th
CENTRAL PARK
HUDSON RIVER
West End Av
Central Park West
Central Park East
Madison Av
Park Av
Lexington
Third Av
Second Av
First Av
5
W 72nd
E 72nd
13
Broadway
WEST CHANNEL
EAST CHANNEL
9
QUEENSBORO BRIDGE
Central Park South
East River Dr
7
6
Henry Hudson Pkwy
W 42nd
E 42nd
QUEENS MIDTOWN TUNNEL
3
Avenue of the Americas
W 34th
E 34th
EAST RIVER
Eleventh Av
Tenth Av
Ninth Av
Eighth Av
1
Fifth Av
Madison Av
Park Av
Lexington
Third Av
Second Av
First Av
W 23rd
E 23rd
12
W 14th
E 14th
Fourth Av
Av A
Av B
Av C
Av D
8
Christopher St
6th Av
11
4
E Houston St
W Houston St
Delancy St
Greenwich
Jackson St
HOLLAND TUNNEL
10
Canal St
Grand St
E Broadway
Broadway
Bowery
Church St
Chambers
Fulton St
MANHATAN BRIDGE
Liberty St
BROOKLYN BRIDGE
Wall St
FDR Dr
2
BATTERY PARK
BROOKLYN

50

ROOM WITH A LOO

There was a time when people used the subway restrooms. Really.

Today, finding a safe, clean public facility—that won't cost you a fifteen dollar sit-down lunch—can be a challenge.

The following list should help. All restrooms are in building lobbies or public areas.

1 875 Third Ave. at 52nd St.
M-Sat, 7am-11pm;
Sun, 11am-7pm

2 Avery Fisher Hall
Lincoln Center
Daily, 10am-11:30pm

3 Central Research Library
New York Public Library
Fifth Ave. bet. 40th and
42nd Sts.
Men: 3rd Floor;
Women: 1st Floor
M-Thur, 9am-9pm;
F and Sat, 10am-6pm

4 Citicorp Center
153 East 53rd St.
M-F, 7am-midnight;
Sat-Sun, 8am-midnight

5 City University Graduate
Center
33 West 42nd St.
M-F, 8am-10:30pm;
Sat, 9am-5pm

6 Crystal Pavilion
805 Third Ave. at 50th St.
M-Sat, 8am-11pm

7 Forbes Building
Fifth Ave. at 12th St.
Tue-Sat, 10am-4pm

8 Hunter College
Lexington at 68th St.
Daily, 8am-9pm

9 IBM Garden Plaza
590 Madison Ave.
Daily, 8am-10pm

10 Library and Museum for the
Performing Arts
111 Amsterdam Ave. or
Lincoln Center Plaza North
M and Th, 10am-8pm;
Tue, W, and F, noon-6pm;
Sat, 10am-6pm

11 Marriott Marquis Hotel
1535 Broadway at 45th St.
Daily, 24 hours

12 Olympic Tower
Fifth Ave. bet. 51st and 52nd
Sts.
Daily, 7am-midnight

13 Park Ave. Plaza
55 East 52nd St.
Daily, 8am-10pm

14 Parker Meridien Atrium
118 West 57th St.
Daily, 7am-midnight

15 RCA Building
30 Rockefeller Plaza
Fifth Ave. bet. 50th and 51st St.
M-F, 10am-7pm;
Sat-Sun, 10am-6pm

16 Trump Tower
725 Fifth Ave.
Daily, 10am-7pm

17 Waldorf-Astoria Hotel
Park Ave. at 50th St.
Daily, 24 hours

18 Whitney Museum of Art at
Philip Morris
Park Ave. at 42nd St.
M-Sat, 7:30am-9:30pm;
Sun, 11am-7pm

19 World Financial Center
Winter Garden
West St. entrance
Daily, 6am-11pm

20 World Trade Center
Concourse
Near PATH trains
Daily, 24 hours

ACKNOWLEDGEMENTS

We are deeply grateful to the following people whose contributions have made this book possible.

Hervé Aaron
Donald Albrecht
Francesco Antonucci
Richard Baron
Billie Billing
Joan Brown
Michele Cohen
Katherine Cowles
Dina De Luca
Jackie Drexel
Gwendolyn Dunaif
Nina Duran
Joel Fram
Jerry Gold
Paul Goldberg
Bill Harris
Geoffrey Holder
Thomas Hoving
Miles Jaffe
André Jammet
Erica Kaplan

Fred Lebow
David Levy
Anthony Paul
Rosemarie Robotham
Irene Rubano
Peter Schaffer
Martha Stewart
Timothy White
Judith Yeargin

…and to the following organizations

The Central Park Zoo
The Russian Tea Room
The South Street Seaport
New York Road Runners Club
The Metropolitan Museum of Art
The New York Transit Authority

50 MAPS OF NEW YORK

Credits

Istvan Banyai: 23
Yvonne Buchanan: 47
George Colbert: 35
Nina Duran: 1, 13
Floor Plans, courtesy of the Metropolitan Museum of Art: 19
Steven Guarnaccia: 16
Janine Leib: title page map
Marathon Map, courtesy of the New York Road Runners Club: 34

Hélène Maumy-Florescu: 3
Marc Rosenthal: 40, 41, 42
Seaport Map, courtesy of 212 Associates: 2
J.C. Suarès: 14, 20, 25, 29
Subway Map, courtesy of the New York Transit Authority: 30
Christy Trotter: 48